THE
INUIT

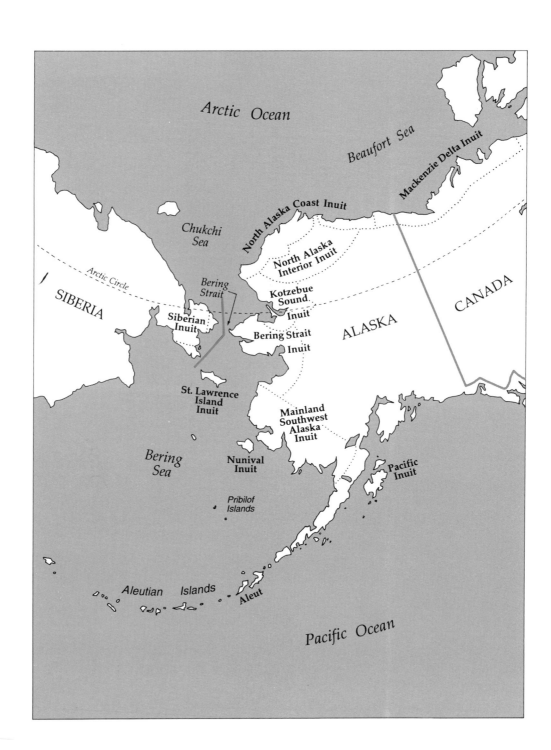

Arctic Ocean

Beaufort Sea

Mackenzie Delta Inuit

Chukchi
Sea

North Alaska Coast Inuit

North Alaska
Interior Inuit

Arctic Circle

Bering
Strait

Kotzebue
Sound
Inuit

SIBERIA

CANADA

Siberian
Inuit

Bering Strait
Inuit

ALASKA

St. Lawrence
Island
Inuit

Mainland
Southwest
Alaska
Inuit

Bering
Sea

Nunival
Inuit

Pacific
Inuit

Pribilof
Islands

Aleutian   Islands

Aleut

Pacific Ocean

THE INUIT

Nancy Bonvillain

Frank W. Porter III
General Editor

CHELSEA HOUSE PUBLISHERS
New York   Philadelphia

On the cover   A plague mask of a northern Alaska or
Bering Sea group.

Chelsea House Publishers
Editorial Director   Richard Rennert
Executive Managing Editor   Karyn Gullen Browne
Copy Chief   Robin James
Picture Editor   Adrian G. Allen
Creative Director   Robert Mitchell
Art Director   Joan Ferrigno
Production Manager   Sallye Scott

Indians of North America
Senior Editor   Sean Dolan
Native American Specialist   Jack Miller

Staff for **THE INUIT**
Editorial Assistant   Annie McDonnell
Assistant Designer   Fran Bonamo
Picture Researcher   Sandy Jones

First Printing

1   3   5   7   9   8   6   4   2

Library of Congress Cataloging-in-Publication Data

Bonvillain, Nancy.
    The Inuit / Nancy Bonvillain; Frank W. Porter III, general
editor.
        p.   cm.—(Indians of North America)
    Includes bibliographical references (p.   ) and index.
    ISBN 1-55546-705-9.
        0-7910-0380-9 (pbk.)
    1. Inuit—Social life and customs—Juvenile
literature.   2. Arctic regions—Social life and customs—
Juvenile literature.   [1. Inuit.   2. Eskimos.]   I. Porter, Frank
W., 1947–   .   II. Title.   III. Series.
E99.E7B685   1995   94-42470
971'.004971—dc20   CIP
                                                          AC

CONTENTS

INDIANS OF NORTH AMERICA

The Abenaki

The Apache

The Arapaho

The Archaeology
  of North America

The Aztecs

The Blackfoot

The Cahuilla

The Catawbas

The Cherokee

The Cheyenne

The Chickasaw

The Chinook

The Chipewyan

The Choctaw

The Chumash

The Coast Salish Peoples

The Comanche

The Creeks

The Crow

Federal Indian Policy

The Hidatsa

The Hopi

The Huron

The Innu

The Inuit

The Iroquois

The Kiowa

The Kwakiutl

The Lenapes

Literatures of the
  American Indian

The Lumbee

The Maya

The Menominee

The Modoc

The Mohawk

The Nanticoke

The Narragansett

The Navajos

The Nez Perce

The Ojibwa

The Osage

The Paiute

The Pawnee

The Pima-Maricopa

The Potawatomi

The Powhatan Tribes

The Pueblo

The Quapaws

The Sac and Fox

The Santee Sioux

The Seminole

The Shawnee

The Shoshone

The Tarahumara

The Teton Sioux

The Tunica-Biloxi

Urban Indians

The Wampanoag

Women in American
  Indian Society

The Yakima

The Yankton Sioux

The Yuma

The Zuni

CHELSEA HOUSE PUBLISHERS

INDIANS OF NORTH AMERICA:
CONFLICT AND SURVIVAL

Frank W. Porter III

*The Indians survived our open intention of wiping them out, and
since the tide turned they have even weathered our good intentions
toward them, which can be much more deadly.*

John Steinbeck
America and Americans

When Europeans first reached the North American continent, they found
hundreds of tribes occupying a vast and rich country. The newcomers quickly
recognized the wealth of natural resources. They were not, however, so quick
or willing to recognize the spiritual, cultural, and intellectual riches of the
people they called Indians.

The Indians of North America examines the problems that develop when
people with different cultures come together. For American Indians, the
consequences of their interaction with non-Indian people have been both
productive and tragic. The Europeans believed they had "discovered" a "New
World," but their religious bigotry, cultural bias, and materialistic world view
kept them from appreciating and understanding the people who lived in it.
All too often they attempted to change the way of life of the indigenous
people. The Spanish conquistadores wanted the Indians as a source of labor.
The Christian missionaries, many of whom were English, viewed them as
potential converts. French traders and trappers used the Indians as a means
to obtain pelts. As Francis Parkman, the 19th-century historian, stated, "Spanish civilization crushed the Indian; English civilization scorned and neglected
him; French civilization embraced and cherished him."

7

Nearly 500 years later, many people think of American Indians as curious vestiges of a distant past, waging a futile war to survive in a Space Age society. Even today, our understanding of the history and culture of American Indians is too often derived from unsympathetic, culturally biased, and inaccurate reports. The American Indian, described and portrayed in thousands of movies, television programs, books, articles, and government studies, has either been raised to the status of the "noble savage" or disparaged as the "wild Indian" who resisted the westward expansion of the American frontier.

Where in this popular view are the real Indians, the human beings and communities whose ancestors can be traced back to ice-age hunters? Where are the creative and indomitable people whose sophisticated technologies used the natural resources to ensure their survival, whose military skill might even have prevented European settlement of North America if not for devastating epidemics and disruption of the ecology? Where are the men and women who are today diligently struggling to assert their legal rights and express once again the value of their heritage?

The various Indian tribes of North America, like people everywhere, have a history that includes population expansion, adaptation to a range of regional environments, trade across wide networks, internal strife, and warfare. This was the reality. Europeans justified their conquests, however, by creating a mythical image of the New World and its native people. In this myth, the New World was a virgin land, waiting for the Europeans. The arrival of Christopher Columbus ended a timeless primitiveness for the original inhabitants.

Also part of this myth was the debate over the origins of the American Indians. Fantastic and diverse answers were proposed by the early explorers, missionairies, and settlers. Some thought that the Indians were descended from the Ten Lost Tribes of Israel, others that they were descended from inhabitants of the lost continent of Atlantis. One writer suggested that the Indians had reached North America in another Noah's ark.

A later myth, perpetrated by many historians, focused on the relentless persecution during the past five centuries until only a scattering of these "primitive" people remained to be herded onto reservations. This view fails to chronicle the overt and covert ways in which the Indians successfully coped with the intruders.

All of these myths presented one-sided interpretations that ignored the complexity of European and American events and policies. All left serious questions unanswered. What were the origins of the American Indians? Where did they come from? How and when did they get to the New World? What was their life—their culture—really like?

In the late 1800s, anthropologists and archaeologists in the Smithsonian Institution's newly created Bureau of American Ethnology in Washington,

D.C., began to study scientifically the history and culture of the Indians of North America. They were motivated by an honest belief that the Indians were on the verge of extinction and that along with them would vanish their languages, religious beliefs, technology, myths, and legends. These men and women went out to visit, study, and record data from as many Indian communities as possible before this information was forever lost.

By this time there was a new myth in the national consciousness. American Indians existed as figures in the American past. They had performed a historical mission. They had challenged white settlers who trekked across the continent. Once conquered, however, they were supposed to accept graciously the way of life of their conquerors.

The reality again was different. American Indians resisted both actively and passively. They refused to lose their unique identity, to be assimilated into white society. Many whites viewed the Indians not only as members of a conquered nation but also as "inferior" and "unequal." The rights of the Indians could be expanded, contracted, or modified as the conquerors saw fit. In every generation, white society asked itself what to do with the American Indians. Their answers have resulted in the twists and turns of federal Indian policy.

There were two general approaches. One way was to raise the Indians to a "higher level" by "civilizing" them. Zealous missionaries considered it their Christian duty to elevate the Indian through conversion and scanty education. The other approach was to ignore the Indians until they disappeared under pressure from the ever-expanding white society. The myth of the "vanishing Indian" gave stronger support to the latter option, helping to justify the taking of the Indians' land.

Prior to the end of the 18th century, there was no national policy on Indians simply because the American nation had not yet come into existence. American Indians similarly did not possess a political or social unity with which to confront the various Europeans. They were not homogeneous. Rather, they were loosely formed bands and tribes, speaking nearly 300 languages and thousands of dialects. The collective identity felt by Indians today is a result of their common experiences of defeat and/or mistreatment at the hands of whites.

During the colonial period, the British crown did not have a coordinated policy toward the Indians of North America. Specific tribes (most notably the Iroquois and the Cherokee) became military and political pawns used by both the crown and the individual colonies. The success of the American Revolution brought no immediate change. When the United States acquired new territory from France and Mexico in the early 19th century, the federal government wanted to open this land to settlement by homesteaders. But the Indian tribes that lived on this land had signed treaties with European governments assuring their title to the land. Now the United States assumed legal responsibility for honoring these treaties.

At first, President Thomas Jefferson believed that the Louisiana Purchase contained sufficient land for both the Indians and the white population. Within a generation, though, it became clear that the Indians would not be allowed to remain. In the 1830s the federal government began to coerce the eastern tribes to sign treaties agreeing to relinquish their ancestral land and move west of the Mississippi River. Whenever these negotiations failed, President Andrew Jackson used the military to remove the Indians. The southeastern tribes, promised food and transportation during their removal to the West, were instead forced to walk the "Trail of Tears." More than 4,000 men, woman, and children died during this forced march. The "removal policy" was successful in opening the land to homesteaders, but it created enormous hardships for the Indians.

By 1871 most of the tribes in the United States had signed treaties ceding most or all of their ancestral land in exchange for reservations and welfare. The treaty terms were intended to bind both parties for all time. But in the General Allotment Act of 1887, the federal government changed its policy again. Now the goal was to make tribal members into individual landowners and farmers, encouraging their absorption into white society. This policy was advantageous to whites who were eager to acquire Indian land, but it proved disastrous for the Indians. One hundred thirty-eight million acres of reservation land were subdivided into tracts of 160, 80, or as little as 40 acres, and allotted tribe members on an individual basis. Land owned in this way was said to have "trust status" and could not be sold. But the surplus land—all Indian land not allotted to individuals—was opened (for sale) to white settlers. Ultimately, more than 90 million acres of land were taken from the Indians by legal and illegal means.

The resulting loss of land was a catastrophe for the Indians. It was necessary to make it illegal for Indians to sell their land to non-Indians. The Indian Reorganization Act of 1934 officially ended the allotment period. Tribes that voted to accept the provisions of this act were reorganized, and an effort was made to purchase land within preexisting reservations to restore an adequate land base.

Ten years later, in 1944, federal Indian policy again shifted. Now the federal government wanted to get out of the "Indian business." In 1953 an act of Congress named specific tribes whose trust status was to be ended "at the earliest possible time." This new law enabled the United States to end unilaterally, whether the Indians wished it or not, the special status that protected the land in Indian tribal reservations. In the 1950s federal Indian policy was to transfer federal responsibility and jurisdiction to state governments, encourage the physical relocation of Indian peoples from reservations to urban areas, and hasten the termination, or extinction, of tribes.

Between 1954 and 1962 Congress passed specific laws authorizing the termination of more than 100 tribal groups. The stated purpose of the termination policy was to ensure the full and complete integration of Indians into American society. However, there is a less benign way to interpret this legislation. Even as termination was being discussed in Congress, 133 separate bills were introduced to permit the transfer of trust land ownership from Indians to non-Indians.

With the Johnson administration in the 1960s the federal government began to reject termination. In the 1970s yet another Indian policy emerged. Known as "self-determination," it favored keeping the protective role of the federal government while increasing tribal participation in, and control of, important areas of local government. In 1983 President Reagan, in a policy statement on Indian affairs, restated the unique "government is government" relationship of the United States with the Indians. However, federal programs since then have moved toward transferring Indian affairs to individual states, which have long desired to gain control of Indian land and resources.

As long as American Indians retain power, land, and resources that are coveted by the states and the federal government, there will continue to be a "clash of cultures," and the issues will be contested in the courts, Congress, the White House, and even in the international human rights community. To give all Americans a greater comprehension of the issues and conflicts involving American Indians today is a major goal of this series. These issues are not easily understood, nor can these conflicts be readily resolved. The study of North American Indian history and culture is a necessary and important step toward that comprehension. All Americans must learn the history of the relations between the Indians and the federal government, recognize the unique legal status of the Indians, and understand the heritage and cultures of the Indians of North America.

The Inuit occupy the Arctic regions of Alaska and Canada. This photograph of an Inuit woman was taken in Nome, Alaska, in 1908.

ANCESTORS

The Inuit (IN-u-it) live in a unique and forbidding environment. Inuit communities are located throughout the Arctic from the western Pacific coast of Alaska to the eastern Atlantic shores of Canada. Theirs is a vast territory, spreading more than 4,000 miles through six time zones. Today numbering more than 60,000, the Inuit in Alaska and Canada are united by similarities in culture and history.

Temperatures in the Arctic vary somewhat across the enormous expanse of land. Daily temperatures in the coldest month of January range from a low of -30 or -35 degrees Fahrenheit in central and eastern Canada to a high of 0 or 10 degrees Fahrenheit in western Alaska. Average temperatures in the warmest summer month of July range from a low of 35 or 40 degrees Fahrenheit in central and eastern Canada to a high of 50 or 55 degrees Fahrenheit in western Alaska. Despite some warming in the summer, Arctic ground remains frozen throughout the entire year because of long, intensely cold winters.

Annual rates of snowfall in the Arctic are relatively light considering the region's northern location. They average from 40 to 65 inches in the western Arctic to 45 to 125 inches in the eastern. But since the ground is frozen and the air is continuously cold, little or no snow melts or seeps into the earth to drain underground. Ice begins to form on lakes and rivers early in autumn. By the middle of October, many inland waterways are completely frozen. The ice does not usually begin to clear until early in June and often is not completely melted until the end of June or beginning of July.

The difficulties of living in the Arctic environment led to many special developments in the culture of the Inuit. The people survived in extreme cold by inventing a unique technology for making clothing and building houses that retain as much heat as possible. They coped with a scarcity of resources by living in small communities and gaining a broad knowledge of the habits of animals that they depend upon for food.

Several species of marine mammals, such as seals, walrus, and whales, supply a major portion of the annual diet of Inuit living near the coast. The Inuit's diet also includes freshwater fish such as Arctic char, salmon, lake trout, whitefish, and pike.

A number of species of land animals enter inland Arctic territory during their seasonal migrations. Among these are the caribou, bear, wolf, musk ox, fox, weasel, and squirrel. Birds such as the raven, snowy owl, and some water and shore birds also make their appearance in the Arctic during summer migrations.

Although there are a variety of food sources in the Arctic, the animals, fish, and birds appear in limited supply and only during specific seasons of the year. Because of these limitations, the Inuit pay close attention to the migration patterns and behavior of marine and land animals in their region. The Inuit learn the annual migration cycles followed by whales, caribou, and birds. They know when these species will arrive and can then plan their hunting activities. The Inuit are also keenly aware of seasonal changes in the supply of sea mammals such as seals and walrus and of the varieties of fish in Arctic waters.

Prior to the modern period, the lifestyle of the Inuit was highly mobile. They utilized their resources intensively whenever they were available. Seasonal changes in the movements and supply of animals led to relocations of Inuit settlements. Since the people depended on food resources that were themselves mobile, the Inuit had to be ready to move their camps and villages to places closest to the animal populations. The Inuit therefore needed to know conditions of the land in a vast area in order to best exploit the resources throughout the year. When traveling or hunting on ice and snow, they needed to know weather conditions, the thickness of ice, and the likelihood of finding animals in specific places.

In addition to cultural adaptations that the Inuit have made to the Arctic, over many centuries their bodies have adapted to living in an extremely cold environment. The major problem presented by living in the Arctic is the need to preserve body heat. Most important is protection of the central core of the body, including the outer skin of the chest and back and the internal organs. Loss of body heat, a condition called hypothermia, can be fatal. Prolonged cold in the arms and legs can lead to frostbite, which can also cause death.

The bodies of Inuit people have made several specific adjustments to improve their chances for survival. Recent scientific studies show that the metabolism of the Inuit produces a greater amount of body heat than does that of other peoples. Body heat is reflected by a measure known as basal metabolic rate, or the amount of heat produced by a body at rest, when the individual is not engaged in any activity, including digestion. Comparisons of basal metabolic rates of the Inuit with those of other groups indicate that the Inuit's rate is from 13 percent to 33 percent higher.

Additional physical adaptations allow the Inuit to respond to their unique climatic conditions. The Inuit have fewer sweat glands in their legs

Nothing has had a greater influence on Inuit culture than the forbidding environment in which they live.

*Most Inuit peoples have in common a religious tradition that emphasizes the role of the
shaman (center), who serves as the link to the spirit world.*

and feet than do other peoples. Since the production of sweat is the body's means of cooling, people who have fewer sweat glands can retain more body heat.

The Inuit generally demonstrate a better physiological response to exposure to the cold than do other groups. Blood vessels in their hands dilate, or expand, when exposed to the cold. Since their blood vessels expand quickly, they are able to carry fresh warm blood rapidly to extreme areas of the body, thus avoiding the dangers of frostbite. The Inuit's hands and fingers stay warmer, rewarm faster, and tolerate the stress of cold better than do those of other peoples.

Another physical adaptation made by the Inuit is their ability to digest the high proportion of animal protein and fats typical of their diet. Theirs is a diet rich in fish and marine and land animals. But although the Inuit eat foods containing high amounts of fats and oils, they have very low rates of ailments such as diabetes and cardiovascular disease. One explanation for low rates of heart and circulatory diseases among the Inuit concerns the types of fats and oils in their diet. Sea mammals, fish, and caribou have polyunsaturated fats that do not lead to high levels of cholesterol in the blood in contrast to the saturated fats contained in most animal sources. In addition, oils from fish may actually help reduce cholesterol in the blood. A second explanation concerns the Inuit's digestive system. Scientific studies show that even when eating the same diet as other people in Canada and the United States, the Inuit absorb cholesterol from foods in a more efficient manner, avoiding the buildup of cholesterol in the blood that can lead to heart ailments and stroke.

All of these physical adaptations are well documented by modern research. But, of course, they developed over thousands of years when the ancestors of the Inuit began to live in the cold environment of the Arctic.

The earliest settlements of people in the Arctic date back some 10,000 years. The climate then was extremely cold and the ground was covered with ice and snow. The first period of Arctic culture, known today as the Paleo-Archaic, lasted from 9000 B.C. to 5000 B.C. At that time, people lived in what is now eastern Alaska. The western regions of Alaska and the vast territory in Arctic Canada were uninhabited.

A number of settlements maintained by ancestors of the modern Inuit have been discovered in eastern Alaska. One of the earliest was the site of Akmak, dated to 8000 B.C. Akmak was situated on a bluff overlooking the Kobuk River and nearby valley. Additional small camps were located along the Kobuk River. The people of Akmak left behind signs of their technology and economy. They used large tools made from a stone called chert. Their tools included various kinds of knives, scrapers, blades, and bows and arrows. The remains of animal hides give evidence of the people's diet. Remains of caribou are the most numerous, although some bison and elk have also been found at Alaskan campsites.

By approximately 6000 B.C., the Arctic climate gradually became somewhat warmer. Ice began to melt, resulting in a slow rising of the seas. This trend continued for thousands of years. The seas reached their present levels by 2000 B.C. Another important environmental trend during this period was the growth of vegetation and woods in interior Arctic areas. Spruce and birch trees became more numerous. And as plants and trees grew farther north, caribou and other woodland animals migrated into the more northerly regions.

The period of climatic change, beginning in 6000 B.C. and lasting until 2000 B.C., was a time of increase in the human population of the Arctic. This second

This coastal Inuit village in the Yukon region of Alaska sits atop an earlier settlement that dates back hundreds of years. Human habitation of the Arctic dates back more than 10,000 years.

STAGES OF INUIT CULTURAL DEVELOPMENT

	Time Period	Alaska	Canada
I	9000–5000 B.C.	Paleo-Archaic	
II	5000–2200 B.C.	Northern Archaic	
III	2200–1200 B.C.	Arctic Small Tool Tradition	Pre-Dorset
IV	1200 B.C.–600 A.D.	Alaskan Thule	Dorset
V	600–1800 A.D.	Prehistoric Inuit	Canadian Thule

period of Arctic development is known as the Northern Archaic. An early Northern Archaic settlement was Tuktu, located in the Brooks Range of eastern Alaska. Tuktu dates from 4560 B.C. The people there evidently hunted caribou. They used many different kinds of tools of various sizes. Large knives, scrapers, and other butchering utensils have been found. The people also made small blades for cutting. They lived in tents made of caribou skins and built fires inside them for cooking and heating. In addition, they had outdoor fireplaces that they used for cooking.

By approximately 4000 B.C., some ancestors of the Inuit resided along the coast of Alaska while others lived in interior regions. The tools and economies of coastal and inland groups were clearly distinct.

The third important stage in the development of Arctic cultures began in approximately 2200 B.C. and lasted until 1200 B.C. By that time, all of the Arctic was inhabited, from the western coast of Alaska and eastward throughout northern Canada. The third period is now called the Arctic Small Tool Tradition. It is so named because one of its most prominent features was the development of highly specialized small tools of various kinds and uses.

The peoples living during this period used tools such as delicate small blades, adzes, scrapers, and knives. Tools were made from highly polished slate and other stones as well as from animal bone and antler. The people's hunting equipment included arrows and spears for hunting land animals and harpoons for marine animals. And they used nets and net sinkers for fishing.

People in Alaska shifted their camps on a seasonal basis from inland regions to the coast. These changes give evidence of the flexible economies of the Inuit's ancestors. The people made use of different resources when they were seasonally available. An early coastal site was that of Cape Denbigh on Norton Sound. People lived at Cape Denbigh during the late spring or summer when seals migrated into the seas near Alaska.

By approximately 1600 B.C., some Alaskan coastal settlements were permanent. People who lived there occasionally traveled inland to hunt caribou and birds but most of their economy was based on hunting sea mammals and polar bears. Peoples living in the interior of the Arctic maintained a nomadic way of life since they depended on migratory animals such as caribou and elk for food.

The houses of the people living during the period of the Arctic Small Tool Tradition were larger than those of previous times. Houses had central hearths used for cooking and heating. Floors were built somewhat below ground level. Winter houses had long, deep entrance passages leading to the main room. Such passages protected the interior of the house from the extreme cold of Arctic winters.

The fourth stage of development in Alaska is called the Alaskan Thule Tradition. It began in approximately 1200 B.C. and lasted until A.D. 600. During this period, coastal Alaskan settlements grew larger and more stable. People made tools that were specifically designed for fishing and hunting sea mammals. They had several kinds of nets, spears, and harpoons. Tools were made of wood, stone, and ivory. The people also made stone lamps that they lit with whale oil.

Toward the end of the Thule period, the people began to make iron utensils. They also used their technology and ingenuity to produce intricate artwork. They made ivory carvings of animals and human beings. These carvings were often etched with geometric designs.

During the Alaskan Thule Tradition, Alaskan coastal settlements grew larger than in previous times. One village, located at Point Hope, contained 600 houses built along ridges on the beachfront. Modern researchers today disagree about whether all the houses were occupied at the same time. In any case, evidence clearly shows that Point Hope was a large, stable community.

The fifth and final ancestral stage of cultural development in Alaska is called the Prehistoric Inuit Tradition. It began in A.D. 600 and lasted until approximately A.D. 1800 when the culture of the modern Inuit began to change as a result of contact with European traders and explorers. During the last prehistoric stage, the people produced an increased variety of tools. Coastal peoples used specialized equipment for hunting seals

These tools and weapons date from the Arctic Small Tool Tradition period of Inuit culture. They include harpoon heads; fish spears; scrapers, blades, and other cutting implements; and a needle. All are made of stone.

and whales. Inland groups focused their economies on hunting caribou.

The people lived in inland and coastal villages containing both single-room and multiroom houses. Some villages were permanent while others were inhabited seasonally depending on the availability of nearby resources.

Alaskan peoples created delicate artwork. In addition to ivory carvings representing animals, birds, and humans, artisans made small dolls of wood and bark.

The stages of cultural development in the Canadian Arctic overlap somewhat with those of Alaska although there were differences in the timing of some sequences. Human beings did not venture into the northern Canadian interior until sometime after 2500 B.C. People from Alaska then traveled east throughout interior regions of the Arctic, spreading as far as the Atlantic shores of Labrador and into Greenland. They brought with them the Arctic small tool tradition that had been developed by that time. In Canada, this first period of culture is known as the Pre-Dorset Tradition. It lasted until approximately 800 B.C.–500 B.C.

Several pre-Dorset sites have been found in eastern Canada on Baffin Island, along the shores of Hudson Bay, and in Labrador. In the summer, the people lived in tents usually made from skins of seals or caribou. Their winter houses had the same deep entrance passages to block the flow of cold Arctic air into the interior of the house as those of the peoples in the Alaskan coastal settlements. Houses were lit and warmed with indoor fires and lamps.

Coastal people used spears and harpoons to hunt sea mammals such as seals, walrus, and whales. Inland peoples hunted with bows and arrows and lances to catch animals including caribou, musk ox, and bears. All groups caught fish and birds in their region. They made tools and utensils from bone, antler, ivory, and wood. And they had lamps and bowls made from soapstone.

Pre-Dorset artisans produced a wide array of objects. They made ivory carvings of animals and humans. Many figures were decorated with geometric designs. The people also made small masks representing human faces.

The second stage of cultural development in the Canadian Arctic is called the Dorset Tradition. It began sometime between 800 B.C. and 500 B.C. and lasted until approximately A.D. 1000. During this time, the central and eastern Arctic climate became colder. The people had to adapt to longer periods of cold, snow, and ice. They built sleds to travel over the snow. The sleds were made of whalebone and driftwood. They were usually eight inches in height and as much as six to eight feet long. Driftwood runners were joined together with four or five slats positioned across the runners. The people made boats called kayaks for hunting and travel on the seas. Kayaks were made of whalebone and wood tightly covered with sealskin.

Dorset peoples adapted their clothing and housing to the cold environment. They used sealskin to make warm, watertight boots and hooded coats called parkas. In the long winters, they lived in houses made from snow cut into blocks and stacked together. Some houses were oval while others were rectangular in shape. In the brief summertime, the people lived in houses made of sod. They were from 8 to 22 feet wide and from 14 to 24 feet long.

The artwork of Dorset peoples expanded in number and variety from that produced by earlier cultures. Dorset artisans made objects from many kinds of materials including ivory, antler, bone, wood, and stone. Artisans produced carvings of small wooden dolls fashioned in the form of human beings and animals such as bears, seals, walrus, whales, caribou, and birds. The people also made masks depicting human faces, some of which were life-size while others were miniature representations.

Sometime after A.D. 1000, Dorset cultures in Canada were replaced by a third stage of development known as the Thule Tradition. This tradition spread from the Alaskan Thule peoples eastward throughout Canada. The Thule Tradition was firmly established in Canada by approximately A.D. 1200. It continued until A.D. 1800 when it developed into modern Inuit culture.

In the early part of the Thule Tradition, the climate grew warmer, resulting in a melting of sea ice. As this happened, whales were able to migrate farther north in the Arctic seas. Coastal people then adapted their technology and economies to emphasize whaling.

Both coastal and inland Canadian groups produced an increased variety of tools, utensils, and other objects. They made bows, arrows, lances, and harpoons for hunting. They had lamps made of soapstone and pottery. And they made many personal objects such as combs, needle cases, beads, pendants, and "snow goggles" worn for outdoor activities in the winter. The goggles were made of wood or bone. They covered the wearer's eyes but had a narrow horizontal slit through which the wearer could look out.

Thule settlements varied in size depending on the season. They were smallest in the winter and somewhat larger in summertime. During the winter, groups of perhaps 10 to 50 people lived together in a village containing from one to four houses. The houses were either round or oval in shape. Inside the houses, people built raised platforms on which they slept. The platforms and floors were paved with stone slabs or pebbles. Interior walls were lined with boulders in order to protect against the outside cold. The houses had long entrance tunnels that were also lined with boulders. Winter houses were made of snow blocks while summer houses were made of sod.

Thule culture continued to develop and expand in complexity through A.D. 1300 or A.D. 1400. People adapted their skills to suit the needs of diverse regional environments. They also traded with members of other communities.

After A.D. 1300 or A.D. 1400, the Arctic climate again became colder. As a result, sea ice formed earlier in the autumn,

This 19th-century American magazine illustration depicts Inuit housing. European and American explorers, traders, and settlers were amazed to discover that native peoples could live comfortably in the Arctic without modern technology.

lasted into the summer, and covered a larger area. Sea mammals such as seals, walrus, and whales became less common in the Arctic seas. People then abandoned some of their coastal settlements and moved inland. They relied less on hunting sea mammals and instead focused their economies on caribou.

During thousands of years of residence in the Arctic, ancestors of the modern Inuit in Alaska and Canada adapted to changing conditions in their environment. Throughout their histories, they developed tools, utensils, housing, and clothing to best utilize their resources and survive in their unique region. When peoples now known as the Inuit later encountered traders and travelers from European countries, they had to adapt to a new set of circumstances. ▲

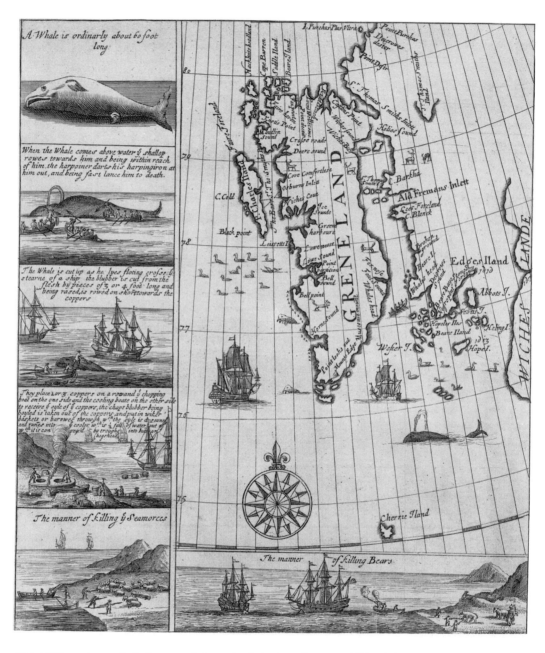

This 18th-century whaler's map of Greenland depicts the way of life of the Inuit who inhabited its western coasts and the animals they relied on as food sources.

INUIT
TRADITIONS

The Inuit's name means *people* in their own language. They reside in a vast territory that provides the setting for diverse ways of living. Although there are numerous regional variations in Inuit culture, the people share many basic traditions.

There are some cultural features that differ from west to east throughout the Arctic. Styles of housing, clothing, food preparation, and artwork may vary in different communities. Other contrasts result from a group's location in either coastal or inland areas. Coastal and inland peoples depend upon local resources for their food. And although most Inuit shift their settlements somewhat between coastal and inland sites on a seasonal basis, communities emphasize one style of living more than the other.

The Inuit do not believe that people have rights to exclusive ownership of specific areas of land, but each community has a general connection to the territory it customarily uses. Since resources are relatively scarce in the Arctic, the people must make full use of whatever animals, fish, birds, and plants are available in their area. They learn the yearly migration patterns of animals and birds. They know where and when supplies of fish and plants are most likely to be found. And the Inuit understand signs of changes in weather conditions and ice and snow formations.

Like their ancestors, the Inuit depend upon a wide array of food sources on a yearly basis, although each type appears for only a relatively short period. The most important marine mammals are seals, walrus, and whales. Ocean and freshwater fish also provide substantial portions of the Inuit diet. Land animals such as caribou and musk ox are caught on the interior tundra of the Arctic. Other land animals, including wolves, foxes, bears, and hares, make a smaller contribution to the food supply.

In all areas, the Inuit catch birds and gather their eggs for food. In summer, people gather blueberries, cranberries, and roots to add fruits and vegetables to their diet.

But despite the people's best efforts to collect all the resources in their region, the Inuit sometimes experience periods of hunger or even starvation. These times are more likely to occur toward the end of the long Arctic winter when animals are scarce and stored food supplies run out. One such tragic episode was recounted in the 1960s by an elderly woman living in northern Quebec in the central Canadian Arctic. Her family's ordeal took place around the turn of the twentieth century. After many days of searching for food, the family of mother, two daughters, and two sons, had to kill their own dogs and eat them. Then, the woman said, as quoted in Nelson Graburn's *Eskimos Without Igloos*:

We were very hungry, going on day after day. My older brother and his wife got a caribou at their place. So he brought us some small pieces of meat. Even then, it was not enough. My married older sister and her husband also brought us some food, eating little themselves. They moved off again to another place to get some food. We kept on moving again. We used a polar bear skin dragging it along as a sled with no dogs left. Other people were abandoning their own children. Then we got one ptarmigan. Eating one ptarmigan—that was hardly enough for everyone. My mother was cutting up her clothes to eat, hats, hoods, and all. We kept on having this for food every time we stopped. We nearly didn't have any clothes left, just enough to keep us warm.

My brother kept on falling down because he was so weak. Then they caught one caribou, but we could still hardly walk from being so thin. We started running out of food again, we left my older sister behind and then our older brother left us behind.

Finally we arrived at Sugluk [a village on the coast] as the snows were beginning to melt, and we were not starved again.

Such desperate times did not come frequently, but the Inuit knew that starvation and death were always possible. As a result, they knew it was crucial to learn as much as they could about the environment and the animals inhabiting it. This knowledge enabled them to survive.

Inuit women and men traditionally divide the necessary work to support themselves and their households. Men do most of the hunting. They use different methods to catch sea and land animals. They pursue seals and walrus in kayaks. These kayaks accommodate one or two people. They are made of driftwood and whalebone wrapped all around with a waterproof sealskin cover. The top of the cover has a hole large enough for a person to sit inside. When a hunter nears the seal or walrus, he attacks it with a lance or harpoon.

Inuit men also hunt seals by finding their breathing holes on the sea ice. Although seals spend most of their time under water, they have to come to the surface periodically to breathe fresh air. Seals make small holes in the sea ice and return to these places when they need to breathe. Inuit hunters locate the breathing holes, often with the help of their dogs, which have a keen sense of smell. Then they position themselves above the breathing hole and wait for a seal to return. Since there is no guarantee that a seal will come to any particular breathing hole, several men usually hunt at breathing holes in a cooperative effort. Each hunter chooses a breathing hole within an area and waits for a seal to appear. Hunters may wait for many hours and still be unsuccessful. If a seal comes to the breathing hole, the hunter uses a harpoon to catch the animal. Then other nearby hunters come to help drag the heavy seal onto the surface of the ice.

Hunting for whales is always a cooperative task. One man has the position of *umialik,* or whaling-crew leader. The umialik owns the equipment needed to hunt whales, including a whaling boat called an *umiak.* An umiak is an open boat made of driftwood and whalebone. It is usually 15 or 20 feet in length and 3 feet deep. The sides and bottom of the boat are covered with sealskin in order to keep water from seeping inside. Men use paddles to steer and propel the boat.

An umialik organizes a whaling crew of 7 to 10 men. Crew members are often, but not always, relatives of the umialik. At the start of the whaling season in early spring, the umialik's wife provides the crew with a new set of clothing that she has made. Then the men set out in the umiak in pursuit of whales on the open sea. When they near a whale, they begin to throw harpoons into its flesh.

Inuit hunt walrus on the thin sea ice between floes. When a walrus broke through the ice to breathe, it was harpooned.

Female Inuit with a long coil of walrus gut. Women accompanied men on hunting expeditions because their domestic skills were essential to their family's survival.

They all help pull the animal close to the boat and finally kill it with lances. The whale is then dragged to shore. The men cut the whale into pieces and carry the meat, bones, and oil back to their village.

When hunters return to their village with meat from sea mammals, they distribute it to members of their community. If a single hunter catches the animal, he distributes its meat, but if several men cooperate in hunting, the man who first harpoons the animal takes charge. Portions of meat are given out according to specific rules. For example, seal meat is distributed in the following manner:

Animal Part	Recipient
Head, eyes, forelimbs, thoracic vertebrae, heart	Women
Cervical and lumbar vertebrae	Men
Ribs, sternum, and attached meat	Hunter who killed it

| Lumbar meat | Men in the hunting party |
| Sacral and caudal vertebrae, hind flippers | Cooked in broth and eaten by all |

The Inuit hunt land animals along the coast and in interior regions. Coastal groups catch polar bears on the ice by approaching the animal when it is asleep. The Inuit dogs surround the bear and hold it at bay while the hunter shoots it with arrows or attacks it with a lance.

Inuit men also hunt caribou, musk ox, bears, wolves, foxes, and hares. Caribou hunting is done singly and cooperatively. Often an entire community takes part in caribou drives, especially in the fall when caribou are most numerous. At that time, the caribou are also most valuable to the Inuit because the animals have fattened over the spring and summer. In addition, the caribou's coats are thick in the fall and therefore best for making clothing, tents, bedding, and other household items.

Men, women, and children participate in a caribou drive. First, the people place stones and boulders in two lines forming a path leading to a pit where hunters await the caribou. Then women and children chase after the caribou, keeping them between the rows of boulders. As the animals near the end of the drive, hunters shoot at them with bows and arrows or attack them with lances. Many animals can be killed at once this way.

The Inuit value products of sea and land animals for many purposes in addition to their use as food. Seal and caribou skins are made into clothing, bedding, and containers. Sealskin is used to cover boats and to cover doorways and windows in winter houses. Caribou skins are used as tents for summer shelters.

Bones and antlers from caribou are made into many different tools and utensils, including spades, scrapers, handles for tools, arrowheads, blades, knives, hooks, and needles. The internal guts of caribou and seals are used for thread and twined rope.

Whalebone is also extensively utilized by the Inuit. It forms the frame of kayaks, umiaks, and sleds. It is used for making tools and utensils. And the Inuit use whale oil for cooking and for lighting their lamps.

The Inuit depend on many other food sources in addition to sea and land animals. Both men and women fish in coastal waters and inland lakes and rivers. They especially prize salmon, Arctic char, and whitefish. The Inuit catch some fish by hooks and lines or by spears. Other fish, such as salmon and char, are caught in traps or nets spread out across streams.

Women and men also catch birds, including seagulls, ducks, and geese, using bows and arrows, darts, and traps. The Inuit also collect birds' eggs from nests along the coast and inland rookeries.

Finally, Inuit women gather plants and fruits when available during the brief Arctic summer. The people particularly like blueberries, cranberries, and several kinds of roots such as young willow root and knotweed. However, due to the short growing season, these foods make only a small contribution to the Inuit's yearly diet.

In addition to women's participation in hunting, fishing, and gathering, they have many other tasks. They prepare daily meals, almost always consisting of meat or fish. Women usually prepare one large meal each day, to be eaten in the late afternoon or evening. Leftovers are eaten as small snacks the next day.

Inuit women use a variety of methods to cook and preserve food. Meat from sea or land animals is boiled in oil, roasted, or allowed to partially decay before eating. Fish is eaten either raw or stored first in ice or snow. The Inuit eat berries either fresh or frozen. Roots are usually boiled in oil and then combined with meat or fish.

Since the animals caught and eaten by the Inuit are often too large for a family's immediate needs, women preserve a surplus that can later be used when fresh foods are scarce. The simplest preservation technique is to bury meat, fish, or berries in an "ice cellar" dug into the frozen ground in a storage area of the house. Inuit women also preserve fish and meat by a process called "smoking." In this process, women first cut the fish or meat into strips and hang it over a small fire. Smoke from the fire slowly cures the meat and keeps it from decaying.

Inuit women are responsible for making all the clothing worn by their families. Women's and men's clothing differs somewhat, although the basic garments are similar in function and styling. Men and women both wear undergarments and outer clothing made of skins from seals or caribou. Undergarments are made with the fur turned inward and outer clothing with the fur turned outward. Undergarments consist of shirts, pants, and stockings. Outer clothes include a hooded parka, although the style of parka differs for women and men. Women's parkas have hoods big enough to accommodate a mother and her baby, whom the Inuit mother carries on her back. Inuit men wear long outer pants while the women wear a wider style similar to culottes. Both women and men wear knee-high boots, stockings, and mittens.

When inside their houses, and outside during the brief summer, the Inuit shed their outer garments and wear their underclothing with the fur turned out.

Since women make clothing from animal skins, the skills required to prepare hides for sewing are extremely important. The process is arduous and time consuming. It is also critical to the people's survival because skins and seams must be completely airtight and waterproof in order to protect the wearer from the bitter cold of Arctic air, snow, and water.

In preparing sealskin, a woman must first cut the skin off a carcass, taking great care not to make tears or holes in it. If any tears occur, she must sew them securely so that no air, and especially no water, can seep through. Then she

The Inuit used light tents to make their summer camps, as shown in this 1881 photograph. Seal carcasses lie on the beach, where an umiak—an open boat designed to be sailed by more than one person—has been drawn up nearby.

Snowshoes and hunting and cooking equipment line the interior passage to the living area of an Inuit winter house.

scrapes off the blubber attached to the inner side of the skin. The skin is washed with snow or rubbed with pebbles to make it smooth. The woman next spreads the skin on pegs in the ground, perhaps an inch aboveground, to allow air to circulate under the skin. In the summer or early fall, the skin is dried in the warm sun and remains soft and pliable. If new clothing is made in the winter, the sealskin is dried over lamps. However, Inuit women only make clothing in the winter in emergencies because the process of drying the skin in winter leaves it hard.

When the skin is dried, the woman cleans it again with a sharp scraper to eliminate any remaining blubber or residue. Then she soaks it in saltwater and next proceeds to wash, dry, and scrape it one last time. The skin is then finally ready to be shaped and sewn into clothing. Women also use the animal skins to make bedding, covers for boats, and various kinds of bags and containers.

In traditional times, most Inuit settlements were seasonal. People changed their locations depending upon the availability of resources. The two major changes occurred in the winter and summer. Throughout most of the Arctic, the Inuit set up winter camps on the ice formed over the seas. There they lived from October or November until sometime in May. Winter camps were the larger of Inuit seasonal settlements. Perhaps 50 to 100 people resided in a single community.

During the winter, the Inuit lived in two types of dwellings. One was a house made of sod. It was usually oval in shape. The size of sodhouses varied, but they could accommodate several related families. The people entered the house through a long passageway that could be as much as 20 feet long. At the end was a small doorway covered with a skin of seal or caribou. The house and passageway were often lined with stones, driftwood, or whalebone in order to protect inhabitants against the winter cold. Along the passageways, people built storage areas to keep their tools, utensils, and hunting equipment. They also stored surplus food in ice cellars dug into the frozen ground.

The Inuit slept on raised platforms or benches built in the rear section of the

Inuit hunters spear salmon. In addition to spears, the Inuit also used nets and traps to capture salmon during their annual summer migrations to the sea.

house. The platforms were covered with warm animal skins. Houses also contained a central fireplace used for cooking and heating. And they had lamps, usually made of soapstone, to provide lighting during the long, dark winters.

A second type of winter house was the igloo made of blocks of snow. Its design was similar to that of sodhouses although igloos were smaller. One or two families lived inside. In some communities, igloos were built close to each other and were joined together with domed passages. People could then visit one another without having to go out into the frigid air.

In the spring and summer, the Inuit changed their locations and their house styles. As sea ice began to melt in May or June, the winter communities dispersed. People separated into small groups, consisting of one or several related families. They moved inland and turned their attention to catching fish and birds and hunting land animals such as caribou and musk ox. They also gathered wild

Though meat and fish constituted virtually all of the Inuit diet, Inuit women did gather berries and nuts during the short spring and summer seasons.

An Inuit woman stitches clothing. Autumn was a particularly important time for such repair work, as it was vital that clothes be air- and watertight for winter.

plants and berries that grew briefly in the summer months.

In the summertime, the Inuit lived in tents made of sealskin or caribou skins. Some of the tents were conical in shape while others were rounded on top. Summer tents were usually smaller than winter houses. They accommodated one or two families. During the summer, peo-

ple made frequent moves to stay close to herds of migrating animals.

Inuit communities along the Alaskan coast tended to be more stable than those in the central Canadian Arctic. In the spring and summer, the Alaskan Inuit remained in their villages and hunted whales that migrated north when the sea ice melted. They hunted on the sea ice

Two Inuit men paddle their kayak to shore at their summer camp. Kayaks were built from a wood or bone frame, which was covered with sealskin to create a waterproof vessel. The only opening was where the paddler sat, thus ensuring that hunting equipment would not be lost or get wet if the boat turned over in the rough Arctic seas. A good kayak was often a family's most valuable possession.

in winter and in the open oceans in summertime.

When moving from place to place, the Inuit relied on their dogs to help carry or pull the people's belongings. Families owned several dogs, perhaps as many as five or six. Dogs were trained to pull the sleds and were harnessed to them in a fan formation with ropes of different lengths. The sleds were packed with the Inuit's many utensils and hunting equipment. They also bore heavy clothing and animal skins used for bedding and housing. During the spring and summer, dogs carried some of the people's possessions on their backs.

Inuit communities are united by strong bonds of kinship. Relatives can depend upon one another for help in daily living and for added assistance in times of trouble. Two or more related families often live together in the same house. They travel together, work cooperatively, and share their food and other resources. When the larger winter villages disperse in the spring and summer, small groups of related people set off and establish temporary camps where they hunt, fish, and gather plant foods. These groups often consist of an older couple and the families of their grown sons. If the parents have died, brothers may form the basis of summer settlements.

Although families united through sisters or through brothers and sisters also may reside together, most Inuit communities are linked by brothers because of the nature of the work that men do. Since men are the hunters and

since hunting in the Arctic often requires cooperation among men, it is advantageous for related men to live and work together.

In small camps of related families, the eldest man is generally recognized as the group's informal leader. In addition to seniority, he must also be an able hunter and be generous, cooperative, and even-tempered.

In larger, more permanent villages, leadership may be exercised by men who excel in hunting. These leaders organize cooperative hunting expeditions. In Alaskan coastal communities, the umialik, or whaling-crew leader, recruits crew members and plans the whale hunts. In inland villages, a skilled hunter takes charge in directing village members engaged in communal caribou drives. But aside from these specific activities, the leaders do not have any authority to control other people.

Inuit communities most often exert informal control over the behavior of their members by gossip and teasing. The Inuit believe strongly that people should be friendly, hospitable, and generous. If an individual does something that goes against Inuit norms, others in the settlement may tease, mock, or insult the wrongdoer. Transgressions include refusal to cooperate with or help someone in need, displays of anger or bad temper, and laziness.

Although the Inuit value peaceful relations among villagers, animosities may develop between individuals. In some Inuit communities, conflicts between men are sometimes settled by a public contest or "song duel." In these cases, the two rivals appear in public and proceed to make up insulting songs about each other. As they take turns and compete to outdo their adversary with creative insult, others in the village witness the contest and respond with laughter. Song duels may not lead to a resolution of the underlying conflict but they can serve to relieve tension between the rivals.

Dangerous antisocial acts such as assaults or murders can lead to feuds and revenge killings. Such crimes are very rare in Inuit communities, but they are treated severely when they do occur. Someone who commits a murder or repeatedly assaults others may be exiled from the settlement. In some cases, members of the village may decide to execute the offender. A man then volunteers or is chosen to carry out the will of the people.

Most Inuit, of course, do not commit offensive acts but rather follow the valued norms of their society. They are taught from childhood to be friendly, good-humored, and cooperative. A child is encouraged to develop these traits by the way she or he is treated. The Inuit shower great affection and care on their children. They teach by example and encouragement rather than by punishment. Inuit adults are playful and indulgent of all children in their household and settlement.

Inuit parents begin to follow rules of behavior toward their children even before the baby is born. When a woman realizes that she is pregnant, she and her husband take steps to ensure that their baby will be healthy. A pregnant woman remains active and moves about as much as possible in order to have an easy delivery and a successful, healthy birth.

Other pregnancy rules have ritual importance. For example, the Inuit believe that both parents should keep knots out of their laces and belts. If knots occur, the Inuit believe that the umbilical cord may strangle the baby as it is born.

Among some Inuit groups, if the parents hope to have a daughter, they face their tent in an inland direction. If they want a son, they face their tent toward the sea.

When a pregnant woman knows that her baby is soon to be born, she goes alone to a separate shelter and awaits the birth. She delivers alone and cuts the umbilical cord herself. The mother then cleanses her baby with a soft skin of a bird.

Inuit babies are given their names immediately after birth. They are usually named after a recently deceased relative of either gender. Inuit names are not gender specific and may therefore be given to either girls or boys.

As Inuit children grow up, they begin to learn the duties they will perform as adults. Young girls and boys imitate their parents' activities. Boys are given toy bows and arrows to practice hunting techniques. They play with miniature sleds pulled by puppies. When they reach the age of 10 or 11, boys begin to accompany their fathers on hunting expeditions.

An Inuit hunter takes aim with his harpoon. Seals, walrus, and whales were important game animals for the Inuit; each could be a most deadly quarry.

Elevated huts such as this one were sometimes used by the Inuit to store meat. They were raised above the ground to protect the provisions from the many carnivorous animals that make the Arctic their home, primarily bears, wolves, and foxes.

Girls help their mothers with household tasks. They learn to cook and sew. And they aid in child care by carrying and tending to younger siblings.

All children, then, acquire the skills usually performed by their own gender. In some families, in addition to learning these duties, daughters or sons may also be taught the tasks associated with the other gender. If a father especially prefers his daughter or if he has no son, a daughter may accompany her father on hunting expeditions and learn all the skills of hunting. If a family has no daughters, parents may teach a son to cook and sew. People who know the full range of duties are later valued as spouses since they have a double set of subsistence skills.

Inuit women and men usually choose their own marriage partners. However, in some communities in central Canada, parents arrange marriages for their sons and daughters when the children are infants. When a couple decides to marry, they simply begin to live together. There is little or no ceremony observed. Parents of the couple may exchange gifts in recognition of the new bond between them.

After marriage, a couple often resides for a time with or near the family of the wife. During this period, the husband helps his parents-in-law and provides food and other services for them. The couple usually remains with the wife's family until the birth of their first child. It may then decide to stay with her kin or move near the husband's relatives.

Through their traditions, Inuit women and men learn the tasks expected of them. They learn how to live peacefully in their communities and how to live successfully in their special environment. ▲

Inuit children learned from a very early age that they shared the world with many other spirits. At birth, each child would be given one or two sacred objects, such as a polar bear's tooth or a caribou's ear. The spirit of those particular animals was believed to look out for the child so long as he or she carried the amulet.

THE
RELIGIOUS
WORLD
OF
THE
INUIT

According to the traditional religion of the Inuit, the world consists of sky and earth. The people believe that at the beginning of existence, the earth was covered with a great flood. The waters gradually receded, exposing dry earth and creating vast oceans. The sky is thought of as a rigid dome resting on the flat earth.

After the earth emerged and seas were formed, human beings were created out of nothingness. The Inuit believe that some animals always existed while others were created by supernatural beings.

The Inuit's religion teaches that the world is inhabited by many kinds of spirits and supernatural beings. Some spirits are associated with natural forms and forces. The sun and moon are thought of as brother and sister. They were originally human but eventually ran up into the sky and became celestial bodies. Thunder and lightning are two sisters who create rain by pouring water from their pails. The stars, winds, and air are also spirit beings.

Other spirits are associated with seas, lakes, mountains, and various natural locations. They guard their domains and can help or harm people traveling in the region.

One of the most important deities is a being who resides in the bottom of the ocean and controls the yearly supply of sea mammals. This deity has different names among different Inuit groups. She is often called Sedna, or "the one from below." Sedna was once a human being. A complex Inuit story tells of her role in the original creation of sea animals. At the end of several ordeals, Sedna's fingers were cut off, fell into the ocean, and were transformed into seals, walrus, and whales. She then sank to the ocean's floor and continues to be responsible for the abundance of sea mammals.

Another major deity is the guardian of caribou. She controls the supply of caribou that migrate through the Arctic each year. Numerous monsters, giants, and dwarfs also dwell in the supernatural realm. These creatures sometimes try to harm people who travel alone in isolated places.

The Inuit believe that all living beings have souls. People have two souls that reside in their bodies when alive. One is called the "breath of life" and the other is "soul." The breath of life disappears when an individual dies. After death, the soul separates from the body but continues to exist. The soul then goes to an afterworld. Souls of most people go to a place inside the earth. Some souls, though, go to an afterworld in the sky. These are souls of women who died in childbirth and of people who died a violent death or committed suicide.

The Inuit show respect to people who have died by following specific rules to prepare and conduct funerals. When death occurs, the deceased's body is wrapped in animal skins and taken outside. In winter, the body is then put in a separate igloo. In warmer weather, it is placed on the ground and covered with rocks or driftwood. The Inuit usually put some possessions of the deceased's inside or on top of the grave. Such items as kayaks, sleds, utensils, and tools may be included. The Inuit believe that the deceased's soul uses these objects in the afterlife. The remainder of the deceased's property is given to his or her children. A woman's possessions are given to her eldest daughter while an eldest son receives goods owned by his father.

Although the Inuit respect their deceased relatives, they also believe that people can be harmed by contact with the dead. If someone dies inside a house, the Inuit protect against contact with the dead by removing the body through a hole made in a wall rather than through the door normally used by the living.

In the Inuit's view, animals are superior to humans in many respects. They are more intelligent, stronger, wiser, and have higher morals. According to the Inuit, animals also have souls. When an animal is killed by a hunter, its soul leaves and takes over the body of another animal.

The relationship between animals and people is complex. People are dependent on animals for survival but animals are not at all dependent on people. Animals show kindness to humans by allowing themselves to be caught. Inuit hunters express gratitude to animals by following certain rituals. When a hunter kills an animal, he honors its soul and thanks it for allowing itself to be caught. The hunter's wife also thanks the animal's soul. When a sea animal is

An Inuit corpse rests on its elevated burial platform. Such platforms protected bodies from predators during a period of ritual mourning and until the ground had thawed enough to permit burial.

killed, the hunter's wife places cold fresh water in the animal's mouth as a token of respect. She honors the soul of a land animal by giving it a small present such as a knife, needle case, or container.

The Inuit are careful to keep separate the products of sea and land. For example, meat from land and sea animals should never be cooked in the same pot at the same time. Seal meat and caribou meat should not be placed next to each other. Seal blood cannot be used to coat arrows used for hunting caribou. And

caribou skins should not be made into clothing when the seal-hunting season begins in early winter.

If people violate these rules, the spirits who protect animals become angry. They then block people's attempts to catch the animals. As a result, people may suffer, starve, and die.

The Inuit's religion teaches the people to follow many rules regarding the spirit world. Hunters perform rituals, recite prayers, and sing songs to ensure a successful catch. Women in pregnancy

A carved grave post marks a burial site.

failure and illness result from violating ritual rules.

When misfortune strikes, people try to better their situation through spiritual and ritual guidance. They seek advice from a specialist called a shaman. Inuit shamans are believed to have many extraordinary abilities. They diagnose and treat illnesses and protect people from harmful spirits; they can predict the future, control the weather, find lost objects, and tell the location of sea and land animals; and they can journey to the supernatural realm, converse with spirits, and bring back messages. Some Inuit believe that shamans can return to life after they have died.

An individual may become a shaman for two different reasons. In some cases, a man or woman may make a deliberate decision to become a shaman. But most often, the individual receives a calling from the spirit world. A spirit appears in the form of a vision and instructs the novice that she or he has special powers and must use them to help other people. The individual then proceeds to seek training from another shaman. She or he learns rituals, prayers, songs, and other skills that are later used in her or his role as healer and intermediary between ordinary people and the spirits. Shamans also learn how to acquire supernatural helpers who assist in rituals and journeys to the spirit realm.

Shamans sometimes act on behalf of their community in contacting spirits and transmitting messages between the spirits and the people. Shamans make yearly journeys to Sedna, the powerful

and childbirth also comply with ritual rules. And all people carry special charms, or amulets, that give them good luck, success, and protection against potentially harmful forces.

The Inuit believe that success, health, and good fortune come from properly carrying out the numerous rituals that surround daily activities. In contrast,

THE STORY OF SEDNA

Long ago there lived an Inuit man and his daughter Sedna. Sedna's mother had been dead for some time. Father and daughter lived a quiet life. Sedna grew up to be a handsome young woman and the youths came from all around to sue for her hand, but none of them could touch her proud heart. Finally, at the breaking up of the ice in spring, a bird flew over the ice and wooed Sedna with enticing song. "Come to me," it said. "Come into the land of the birds where there is never hunger, where my tent is made of the most beautiful skins. You shall rest on soft bearskins. My friends shall bring you all your heart may desire; their feathers shall clothe you; your lamp shall always be filled with oil, your pot with meat." Sedna could not long resist such wooing and they went together over the vast sea. When at last they reached the country of the birds, after a long and hard journey, Sedna discovered that her spouse had shamefully deceived her. Her new home was not built of beautiful pelts but was covered with wretched fishskins, full of holes, that gave free entrance to the wind and snow. Instead of soft caribou skins her bed was made of hard walrus hides and she had to live on miserable fish, which the birds brought her. Too soon she discovered that she had thrown away her opportunities when in her foolish pride she had rejected the Inuit youth. In her woe she sang; "Aja. O father, if you knew how wretched I am you would come to me and we would hurry away in your boat over the waters. The birds look unkindly upon me the stranger; cold winds roar about my bed; they give me but miserable food. O come and take me back home, Aja."

When a year had passed, the father left his country to visit Sedna. She greeted him joyfully and begged him to take her back home. The father heard the outrages endured by Sedna and decided to seek revenge. He killed her husband, took Sedna into the boat, and they quickly left the region. When the other birds found their friend dead and his wife gone, they all flew away in search of the fugitives.

Having flown a short distance, the birds saw the boat and then stirred up a heavy storm. The sea rose in immense waves that threatened the father and daughter with destruction. In this mortal danger, the father decided to offer Sedna to the birds in order to save his own life. He threw her overboard but she clung to the boat with a strong grip. The cruel father then took a knife and cut off the first joints of her fingers. As they fell into the sea they were transformed into whales, the fingernails turning into whalebone. Sedna held on to the boat more tightly but her father cut her fingers at the second joint, and these became seals as they fell into the sea. When the father cut off the stumps of her fingers, they became walrus.

Sedna then sank to the bottom of the ocean where she remains to this day. She took revenge on her father by sending her dogs to where he slept with orders to gnaw off his hands and feet.

Since then, Sedna is the mistress of the seals, walrus, and whales. She lets them swim in the seas so that the Inuit can catch them.

spirit who dwells on the bottom of the ocean and controls the supply of sea mammals. The shaman asks Sedna to provide seals, walrus, and whales so that the people can have a successful hunting season. Some Inuit believe that it is the shaman's soul that travels to the supernatural realm while others think that the shaman's body is transported as well.

The shaman goes on his or her journey to the spirit world during a ritual that is intensely dramatic, made more so by sound effects and ventriloquism produced by the shaman. According to a Danish observer, Knud Rasmussen, who witnessed a shaman's ritual in 1921, the journey proceeds as follows:

> The shaman sits for a while in silence,
> breathing deeply, and then, he
> begins to call upon his helping spirits,
> repeating over and over again: ''The
> way is made ready for me; the way
> opens before me!''

The Inuit believed that both human beings and animals possessed an immortal soul and a conscious mind, enabling a complex series of interactions between the human and animal world, including, in many Inuit tales, transformations from human to animal and vice versa. The lip ornaments worn by these Inuit men serve to make them more closely resemble walrus, whose goodwill the Inuit sought to maintain so as to bring success to the hunt.

When the helping spirits have arrived, the earth opens under the shaman. And now one hears at first under the sleeping place: "Halala-he-he-he, ha-lala-he-he-he!" and afterwards under the passage, below the ground, the same cry. And the sound can be distinctly heard to recede farther and farther until it is lost altogether. Then all know that he is on his way to the ruler of the sea beasts.

Then one hears only sighing and groaning. This sighing and puffing sounds as if the spirits were down under water, in the sea, and in between all the noises one hears the blowing and splashing of creatures coming up to breathe.

The shaman finally arrives at Sedna's dwelling place. At first, Sedna is angry because of people's misdeeds during the previous year. But after the shaman pleads with her, she eventually relents and releases a goodly supply of sea animals for the coming season.

In addition to aiding the community through rituals and prayers, Inuit shaman diagnose and treat illnesses. Shaman employ a combination of observation, knowledge of a patient's personal history, and ritualistic techniques to diagnose medical and psychological problems. And they use a combination of natural remedies and rituals to treat disease.

The Inuit, like all peoples, have a complex theory of disease causation. Some problems have a purely natural cause and can be treated with medical methods. Shamans know how to set broken bones and treat deep wounds resulting from accidents. They also use massage techniques to relax strained muscles. And they know the healing properties of oils derived from fish and animals.

Shamans learn to treat other kinds of problems through ritual. According to the cause-of-disease theories of the Inuit, some illnesses have supernatural causes. People sometimes get sick because they have violated a rule or offended a spirit. When a patient is nervous, agitated, or prone to emotional outbursts, a shaman may likely conclude that the patient's problem has resulted from his or her actions. For example, a hunter may have forgotten to perform a particular ritual before preparing himself to go hunting or the hunter's wife may have neglected to properly thank the animal spirits when her husband brings back seal or caribou meat. In cases such as these, shamans begin treating the patient by first prompting them to recall their wrongdoings. Then, the community gathers together and the patient publicly confesses his or her error. The confession and the community's forgiving response helps the patient by relieving their guilt and anxiety.

The Inuit believe that disease can sometimes be caused by the intrusion of foreign objects into a patient's body. Objects such as small pebbles, animal's teeth or pieces of bone may be shot into someone's body by an angry spirit to retaliate for some wrongdoing or simply from malice. A human witch may also shoot an object into someone in order to do harm. When a patient has a localized pain, stiffness, or burning sensation, the shaman may suspect the presence of a foreign object. In these cases, the shaman must locate the foreign object and extract it. She or he usually does so by massaging and sucking on an inflamed or hardened part of the body where the object is lodged.

Illness can also be caused by "soul loss." The disease of soul loss is connected to the Inuit's theory of sleep and dreams. The people believe that souls

Masks played a very important part in Inuit ceremonial life. Most such masks had their origins in Inuit legends and belief regarding human-animal transformation. Believed to embody spiritual power, Inuit masks also constitute one of the greatest achievements of Native American art.

can leave an individual's body during sleep. They believe that dreams are the adventures experienced by one's soul. As a dream ends, the soul normally returns to the sleeper's body. However, a soul is sometimes unable to return. Perhaps it has gotten lost and cannot find its way back. Or perhaps a malevolent spirit, monster, or witch has captured it and will not allow it to return. Patients who are listless, lack energy and appetite, suffer from insomnia, or lose interest in their normal activities are likely to be victims of soul loss. Cases of soul loss are extremely serious because without a soul a human being will die.

The shaman must find the soul and bring it back to the patient's body. Shamans use their great spiritual powers to search for and retrieve a missing soul. The search takes place during a ritual performed in a darkened house or tent at night. All of the windows and doorways are covered and no light is allowed to burn inside. The shaman stands at the front of the room, the patient lies on the floor nearby, and the rest of the community makes up an attentive and apprehensive audience.

The shaman then proceeds to enter a trance state. She or he calls on spirit helpers to guide and protect him or her on the journey to the supernatural world in search of the missing soul. On the journey, the shaman's soul and spirit helpers come into contact with many evil creatures who try to block their path and force them to turn back. The shaman must do fierce battle with these creatures. In the end, she or he usually defeats them and evades their ambushes. While the shaman is retrieving the lost soul, the audience hears shouts and screams from spirits and monsters in contest over the missing soul. In most cases, the shaman is able to bring the soul back to safety. The patient is then enormously relieved to learn that the soul has been found and returned to her or his body. The patient's energy returns and she or he is able to recover and resume a normal life.

Such cures rely, in part, on the patient's firm belief in the spiritual cause of disease and in the shaman's ability to treat illness by ritual means. They are effective, in part, because of the intense emotional release resulting from the drama of the ritual itself. A patient is understandably terrified at the prospect of dying because the soul is lost. She or he must then depend upon the shaman's courage and skills to retrieve the soul and restore life. In addition, the patient's fear is heightened during the ritual by hearing the battle between the shaman and the malevolent creatures. Finally, when the outcome is successful, the patient experiences enormous psychological relief.

The healing techniques used by Inuit shamans combine the people's knowledge and beliefs about the natural and supernatural realms in which they live. The Inuit rely on their keen observation of events in the natural world to help them survive. And they rely on their religion to help them make sense of events that occur in their daily lives over which they have no direct control. ▲

This Russian engraving, based on a sketch made on July 25, 1790, depicts one of the first encounters between Europeans and Alaskan Inuits.

4

STRANGERS
IN
THE
ARCTIC

In the middle of the 16th century, Inuit living along the eastern coast of Canada encountered European fishermen from France, Portugal, and Spain. The fishermen sailed to North America in the summer months and caught cod and herring in the north Atlantic Ocean around Newfoundland, Labrador, and Quebec. The Inuit, who also fished and hunted seals in coastal waters, met the Europeans and occasionally traded with them.

Relations between the Inuit and Europeans were usually friendly. In some cases, however, hostilities erupted, perhaps because the two groups competed over resources or because the people misunderstood each other's intentions. On one occasion, in 1566, a group of French sailors kidnapped an Inuit woman and child and forcibly took them to Europe. Nothing is now known of the fate of the woman and her child, but the episode certainly gave other

Inuit cause for distrusting European intruders.

Toward the end of the 16th century, European explorers began to venture north into the seas and waterways of the eastern Arctic. They were searching in vain for a northwest passage to China. The first of these voyagers was an Englishman named Martin Frobisher. In 1576, Frobisher sailed along the eastern coast of Baffin Island. He met a number of Inuit on the shores of what is now known as Frobisher Bay. This initial contact turned hostile. Frobisher captured three Inuit men and later brought them to England. In retaliation, the Inuit took five of Frobisher's sailors.

Frobisher was soon followed by other British navigators, many of whom gave their names to waterways and islands in the eastern Arctic. In 1585, John Davis sailed up "Davis Strait" leading to Baffin Island, named after another British explorer, William Baffin. Early in the next century, Henry Hudson made his way through "Hudson Strait" and west to "Hudson Bay." In 1610, Hudson encountered a group of Inuit on Digges Island in the northeast region of Hudson Bay. The Inuit's meeting with Hudson was favorable for both sides. They exchanged gifts and words of friendship.

European traders joined the expeditions into the Arctic. The merchants wanted to establish trade relations with the native peoples. They hoped to obtain furs of animals in the region, especially fox, mink, and beaver.

In 1667, a major step was taken in the European fur trade when the Hudson Bay Company was founded. The company, first known as the Company of Merchant Adventurers into Hudson Bay, was established by two French traders, Pierre Radisson and Medart Chouart des Groseilliers. They obtained financial backing from commercial interests in London. The company began as a small enterprise with a handful of trading posts in northern Canada but eventually played a central role in relations between the native peoples and Europeans. Its commercial operations later had far-reaching effects on the livelihood and lifeways of the Inuit in Canada.

As the British journeyed into the Arctic, the French government also sent explorers and traders into the northern waters of the Atlantic. In 1683, an expedition led by Radisson and des Groseilliers sailed to Hudson Bay and bought sealskin from Inuit living along the coast. Another Frenchman, Louis Jolliet, traveled north along the eastern coast of Labrador and met several groups of Inuit. Jolliet bought sealskin and whale oil from the natives. In his diary, he noted that the Inuit already had obtained a variety of goods from European traders, sailors, and fishermen. They possessed wooden boats and barrels, iron screws, nails, knives, and woven cloth.

During the same period that the British and French were sailing into the eastern Arctic, Russians were exploring the western coasts of Alaska. Russia was separated from the west of North America by a narrow waterway now known as the Bering Strait, named in the 18th century after Vitus Bering, a Danish navigator who was an officer in the Russian Navy. The first Russian voyage to the American Arctic was led by Semen Dezhnev in 1648. After his reports reached the Russian government, Czar Peter the Great sent several expeditions to Alaska to establish trade relations with the native peoples. Russian merchants were mainly interested in obtaining the furs of sea otters for trade to Europe and the Orient.

British, French, and Russian interest in trade with Arctic peoples intensified throughout the 17th and 18th centuries. Both in the eastern and western Arctic, numerous expeditions were undertaken to explore more of the region and seek out native groups. Because of difficulties traveling in Arctic waters, fierce weather conditions, and the isolation of most native communities, many of these journeys were unsuccessful. Some ended in

Drawn by his futile quest for the elusive Northwest Passage, the 16th-century English explorer Martin Frobisher was one of the first Europeans to make contact with the Inuit.

This engraving depicts the Russian settlement established by the fur trader G. I. Shelikhov on Kodiak Island in 1784. The local Inuit soon became accustomed to trading furs to the Russians for the metal and cloth goods they desired.

shipwrecks and deaths from starvation and exposure to the frigid climate. But Europeans continued their voyages to the Arctic because they did not want to give up the possibility of profiting from what they hoped would be a lucrative trade network.

Competition between the British and French in the Arctic increased in the 18th century. In 1717, British traders of the Hudson Bay Company founded a major center named Fort Churchill (now Churchill), on the western coast of Hudson Bay. Smaller posts were also built along the bay.

In the east, the French developed several seal-hunting stations and cod fisheries off the coast of southeastern Labrador in the early 18th century. They hunted seals year-round and fished for cod during the summer from June through September. The Inuit who lived nearby engaged in trade with the French from time to time. Regular trade relations between the two groups began after 1743. In that year, a French team led by Louis Fornel founded a trading post on the Labrador coast. The Inuit brought whalebone and oil to the French and in exchange received manufactured goods, particularly tools and utensils made of metal. The Inuit prized metal items because they were more durable and efficient than objects traditionally made from bone and animal skins.

French and British rivalries in the Arctic ended in 1763 when the French in Canada were defeated by the British after the so-called French and Indian War. Although this conflict did not take place in the Arctic, its outcome had an effect in the region. The French were expelled from Labrador when the territory became a British possession. Relations between the British and Inuit in Labrador began with hostilities. Murders occurred on both sides. Soon a truce was negotiated and the two groups established peaceful relations and resumed the trade that had previously passed between the Inuit and the French.

The British government continued to sponsor exploration of the eastern Arctic coast. And British merchants built additional trading posts in the region. British traders resided at the posts in early summer when sea ice melted. The Inuit came to the stores to exchange their goods for European products. An English explorer, Captain Davison, landed on the north coast of the Hudson Strait in 1786 and noted: "It should be observed that the arrival of the ships is considered by the Inuit as a sort of annual fair; their manufactures of dresses, spears, etc., are reserved for the expected jubilee."

British exploration of the Arctic interior began in the middle of the 18th century. In 1770, a British sailor, Samuel Hearne, was hired by Moses Norton, governor of Fort Churchill, to make the first European overland journey in the northern Arctic. Hearne set out from Fort Churchill on Hudson Bay, proceeded north along the river Coppermine, and finally arrived at the shores of the "Arctic Sea" in the northern reaches of North America. Hearne was guided on his two-year journey by American Indians belonging to a group called "Chipewyan." Along the way, he met several encampments of Inuit and wrote descriptions of some of their traditions in his journal. A number of the encounters between the Inuit and Hearne's party proved disastrous because of hostility between the Inuit and Hearne's Chipewyan guides. At least one group of Inuit was massacred by the Chipewyan.

When the Hudson Bay Company began its commercial operations in the Arctic, traders usually remained at their trading posts and exchanged goods with Inuit who traveled to the stores. But in the later years of the 18th century, merchants started to send agents into interior regions to make contact and establish trading networks with inland Inuit communities. Although some traders feared the Inuit, relations between the Inuit and the British were generally friendly. Indeed, Moses Norton, governor of Fort Churchill, stated: "I have the vanity to think that if any accident was to happen to the English, I have reason to believe that the Natives would rather assist a man in distress than to do otherwise by him."

Further to the east, British merchants opened up trading posts along the Labrador coast. There the Inuit brought whalebone and blubber to exchange for European goods and a few European foods such as flour, tea, and sugar. Some of the traders married Inuit women. They and their descendants set up small communities of settlers in the area.

In addition to trade carried out with professional merchants, the Inuit exchanged their goods with sailors aboard European ships. Participants informally bargained over terms of trade. In his diary, Captain Davison listed the dealings between his sailors and the Inuit of the Hudson Strait in 1786:

A seal's-skin hooded frock for a knife
A seal's-skin pair of breeches . . . needle
Seal's-skin boots . . . saw
A pair of wooden spectacles . . . one bullet
A pair of white feather gloves . . . two buttons
A fishing lance or spear . . . file

In the middle of the 18th century, the British government also began to send navigators to explore the western coast of the Arctic. James Cook led expeditions between 1776 and 1780 that included travel along the Pacific shores north of Bristol Bay in Alaska. Cook was followed by another Briton, George Vancouver, in 1790 and 1795.

During the same period, the Russians also sponsored expeditions to explore the western coast. Vitus Bering led two separate expeditions in 1728 and 1741. He was followed in 1781 by Grigorii Shelikhov. Bering and Shelikhov sailed along the coast of Alaska where they met native people living on Kayak Island and Kodiak Island. These people belonged to a group known as Aleuts (AL-ee-ut). They traditionally resided on several islands, now called the Aleutian Islands, located in the Bering Strait between Alaska and Russia. Russians also made contact with small groups of Inuit who lived along the northern Alaskan coast.

In 1781, the Russians established their first trading post in Arctic America. The post, built by Grigorii Shelikhov on Kodiak Island, was the beginning of a growing enterprise called the Shelikhov Company. Under its guidance, a small group of Russian merchants and government agents founded a colony on Kodiak in 1784. This group supervised trade with native peoples and organized expeditions into interior Alaska. In 1792, the Shelikhov Company was renamed the Russian-American Company and developed a monopoly on trading enterprises for Russians in Alaska. The com-

Men from Captain James Cook's late-1770s Arctic expedition blast away at a herd of walrus. The introduction of commercial, rather than subsistence, hunting to the Arctic forever changed the way of life of the Inuit.

A fur company trader samples fox furs brought to him by an Inuit hunter. Nothing so hastened the demise of traditional Inuit culture as the people's growing dependence on manufactured trade goods.

pany was granted a charter by the Russian government and given a state-sponsored monopoly in 1799.

The Russian government was aware of expeditions led by Britons near Alaska. They grew suspicious of British intentions in what the Russians considered to be their American possession. Since the Russians wanted to assert their claim to Alaska, they sent additional teams to make further explorations both northward along the coast and inland into the Alaskan mainland.

In response to growing competition, the Russians and British continued to increase their activity in the Arctic. Exploration and trading operations proceeded inland both from the west and the east.

As a result of contact between the Inuit and Europeans, the lives of Inuit people changed. Introduction of European goods was the earliest sign of change. Among the many items that the Inuit obtained from European traders were metal tools and utensils such as knives, nails, hammers, fishhooks, pots, and containers. These replaced the bone, antler, and stone equipment traditionally made and used by the Inuit. The Inuit also acquired European gear such as guns and fishnets. These items gave hunters and fishermen an improved chance of success in their pursuit of game both on land and in the seas.

In response to the conditions of European trade, the Inuit began to alter their economic activities and settlement patterns. In order for the Inuit to obtain the European goods that they wanted, they had to devote more of their time and energy to hunting and trapping the animals that the Europeans desired. Traders in different regions specialized in different resources. Along the eastern coast, French and British traders wanted sealskin and whalebone. In the interior, they wanted furs of beaver, mink, and fox. And in the western Arctic, Russian merchants obtained furs of sea otters, seals, and beavers.

In the early period of trade between the Inuit and Europeans, the shift away from traditional economic activities toward trapping for European merchants was gradual and had little impact on Inuit life and culture. However, it was the beginning of a trend that deepened in the 19th and 20th centuries.

The early years witnessed another trend that started slowly and later had much more serious effects on the Inuit. The people gradually came to rely on European traders for goods that began as luxuries and novelties but then became necessities of life. And as the people depended more on European goods, they spent more of the year traveling to trading posts and remaining nearby. Eventually, traditional seasonal migrations and settlement patterns changed as the Inuit wanted closer and easier access to trading centers.

A tragic result of contact between the Inuit and Europeans was the rapid decline in native populations due to the scourge of epidemic diseases brought into the Arctic by European explorers, traders, and sailors. The organisms that cause smallpox, measles, influenza, and tuberculosis did not exist in North America before Europeans arrived on the continent. Since the Inuit and other Native Americans had no prior contact with these organisms, they had not developed any immunities or resistances to them. Therefore, when the diseases began to appear in North America, they spread rapidly and with deadly force in the vulnerable population. Epidemics erupted at different times throughout the Arctic, often decimating whole communities. An early recorded incident occurred in 1781 among a group of Inuit living near Fort Churchill on Hudson Bay. Approximately nine-tenths of the Inuit in nearby communities died in the outbreak.

By the end of the 18th century, Inuit society slowly began to change. At first, the effects of change were small. But the people started to adjust their patterns of living to new conditions brought about by trade with the Europeans. These adjustments later had much more serious consequences for the Inuit. ▲

An Inuit woman displays traditional jewelry.

BETWEEN
TWO
WORLDS

Contact between the Inuit and Europeans expanded during the 19th century. As Europeans continued to explore more Arctic regions, the Inuit living in interior communities first met and then began to trade with the newcomers. Once European traders and sailors began to stay in the Arctic during the winter as well as the summer months, the Inuit had prolonged contact with them. As a result, trading activities took on greater importance in Inuit society.

Although these trends developed throughout the Arctic, they began at different times in different areas. Europeans had the earliest and strongest impact on the lives of the Inuit who settled near either the eastern or western Arctic coasts. The Inuit living in the interior did not have contact with Europeans until later, some not until the late 19th or early 20th century.

During the 19th century, the British government sent expeditions to explore the Arctic in a bid to solidify British claims to the region. Beginning in 1819, Captain John Franklin led several teams along the Canadian Arctic shores. Franklin and others who followed him later in the century met Inuit groups and established friendly relations with them.

At the same time, the Hudson Bay Company increased its commercial operations in the Canadian Arctic. The company opened several trading posts along the shores of Hudson Bay and in the interior. In 1821, they bought out the North West Company of Montreal, a rival trading firm. The Hudson Bay Company was then able to enlarge its number of stores and strengthen its control over Inuit trading activities. They monopolized trade and set prices and terms of exchange.

The merchants wanted the Inuit to trap animals, especially fox and mink. The Inuit exchanged the furs for European tools, utensils, guns, and ammunition. The Hudson Bay Company standardized the values for furs brought to posts by the Inuit and matched them with values for manufactured goods given in exchange. The values were set in terms of mink pelts. Rates of products given in the middle of the 19th century were:

Inuit Goods	Mink Skins
Fox, silver	10
red	4
white	2
Mink	1
Caribou buck	6
Caribou doe	4

Company Goods	Mink Skins
1 yard of cloth	30
1 blanket	15
1 gun	30
1 pocket knife	1
1 skein of twine	1
1/2 lb. of tobacco	1

By this accounting, an Inuit trapper had to bring in three silver fox pelts in order to receive one yard of cloth or one gun. The Inuit had to trade one mink skin for a pocketknife.

In order to receive more goods, Inuit men increased the time spent trapping animals while Inuit women increased their efforts preparing the skins for market. Some people gradually shifted their settlement patterns to be closer to the trading posts.

In many cases, Inuit living near the posts acted as middlemen between traders and the Inuit in more remote regions. They collected furs from the interior groups, exchanged them for goods at the stores, and distributed the goods to the original trappers. This system was in effect by the late 19th century. A Canadian observer of the period, F. F. Payne,

noted: "It is remarkable that, although the Inuit traders carry as many as 30 or 40 parcels of furs owned by different families, they seemed quite able to remember on their return, to whom the goods they obtained in exchange belong, apparently the only note being made by a few marks with their teeth upon some of the articles."

By the middle of the 19th century, European, Canadian, and American whaling operations in the eastern Arctic rapidly expanded. Merchants wanted to obtain whale blubber and bone. Whale blubber was used for lighting lamps and street lights in American and European cities. It was also used for oiling tools and machinery. Whalebone, known as baleen, was extracted from the upper jaw of bowhead whales. It is a material with properties similar to modern plastic. In the 19th century, baleen was used in Europe and North America in the manufacture of corset stays, hoopskirts, buggy whips, umbrella ribs, fishing rods, chair seats, and mattresses.

At first, whaling vessels operated in the Arctic only during the brief summer season. They arrived in July or August and left by early October. During this initial period, the Inuit had relatively little contact with the Europeans. They traded with them aboard ship or at harbor posts along the coast.

Then, beginning in the 1840s, British, Scottish, and American whalers began to stay over during the winter. The whalers remained at harbors on the Atlantic coast of Labrador and Quebec and along the shores of the Hudson Strait and

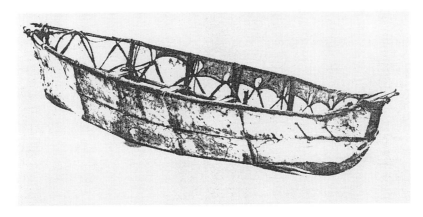

Alaskan Inuit hunters regularly braved the Bering Strait in seemingly flimsy umiaks like this one in search of sea otters and seals.

Hudson Bay. Inuit living nearby developed more regular trade relations with Europeans and Americans at that time. Sailors and whalers obtained food supplies from the Inuit during the long winter months. The Inuit were often employed by the foreigners. They worked as whalers and boatmen aboard the ships. Europeans and Americans also depended on the Inuit for information concerning the regions. The Inuit drew excellent, detailed maps that demonstrated their keen knowledge of the vast territory.

In most cases, relations between the Inuit and Europeans were friendly. One English captain, Leopold McClintock, who commanded an 1859 Arctic expedition, commented: "The Inuit men were stout, hearty fellows, and the women were arrant thieves, but all were good-humored and friendly. There was not a trace of fear, every countenance was lighted up with joy; even the children were not shy, nor backward either, in crowding about us, poking in everywhere."

In contrast, though, some observers described negative aspects of encounters between the Inuit and Europeans. According to a German scientist, Bernhard Hantzch, who traveled with a Canadian fleet in the early 20th century, whaling crews took advantage of Inuit men and women. He wrote: "The whaling crews treated the natives in shameless fashion, betraying the men with a little tobacco, and the women with Branntwein. . . . The poor Inuit yielded themselves to degrading influences, not from badness of character, but from frivolity, good-humoured compliance, and heathenish ignorance."

In some cases, the Inuit were alarmed by Europeans and their technology. The sight of huge ships and the deafening

Kayaks pull up next to an ocean steamer, enabling the Inuit to trade with the passengers onboard.

sound of gunfire caused many people to flee into the interior when the foreigners arrived.

And in other situations, the Inuit felt threatened by the intruders' presence. They saw that Europeans were able to catch a large number of fish with their nets and kill many sea and land animals with their powerful guns. Since the supply of food resources in the Arctic was always limited, the Inuit felt that their own chances of survival were endangered by the large amount of fish and animals taken by Europeans. As a result of competition over scarce resources, some Inuit attacked and killed European whalers, fishers, and hunters who they found in their territory.

In addition, the presence of foreigners in the Arctic threatened the Inuit's survival because of the spread of dangerous diseases of European origin. Epidemics of measles and influenza struck Inuit communities throughout the 19th century. Many people died. And the survivors were terrified by the swift spread and destructive effects of these previously unknown ailments.

In the western Arctic, Russians increased their exploration of Alaska and their trade with the Inuit in the region. In 1818, the Russian-American Company established its first trading post in Inuit territory. Before that time, Russian traders concentrated their operations along the southwestern coast of Alaska in lands inhabited by Aleuts. Russians mainly sought sea otter pelts supplied by the Aleuts, but in the early 19th century, the sea otter population declined considerably because of overtrapping. Then, Russian merchants turned their attention northward and inland to obtain furs of beaver and mink. In these areas, traders came into contact with the Inuit who lived along the northern coast and in the Alaskan interior.

Russian expeditions led by Peter Korsakovsky ventured north of Bristol Bay in 1818 and 1819. They met groups of Inuit who were willing to trap beaver for Russian traders in exchange for manufactured goods. Ten years later, Ivan Vasilev and Fedor Kolmakov explored interior Alaska. They also made contact with the Inuit and set up several trading posts.

In addition to operating trading posts in Inuit territory, Russian merchants traveled to Inuit settlements to make direct contact with the native people. The merchants introduced themselves to community leaders and offered to establish trading partnerships with them. In many cases, the leaders agreed and encouraged other members of their communities to trade with the Russians as well. The Inuit supplied Russians with beaver pelts and in return received iron tools, copper bracelets, glass beads, and some items of clothing.

By the middle of the 19th century, the Inuit were trading regularly with Russian merchants. As in the eastern Arctic, these activities began to have effects on Inuit culture. The people gradually became dependent on traders for manufactured goods that replaced traditional utensils, tools, and weapons.

After 1850, European and American whaling ships expanded their operations into the Arctic waters near Alaska. The Inuit traded with the whalers. Some Inuit also were employed aboard whaling ships and at coastal whaling stations. They were paid in goods such as flour, crackers, tobacco, molasses, matches, guns, and ammunition.

Cultural conflicts sometimes arose between Inuit employees and European and American whalers. According to Inuit beliefs, hunters needed to follow ritual rules in order to ensure a successful catch. Western whalers did not com-

St. Michael's Cathedral in Sitka was a landmark of the Russian Orthodox Church in Alaska. Father Ivan Veniaminov, a Russian Orthodox missionary who converted hundreds of native Alaskans to his faith, oversaw the construction of the cathedral between 1834 and 1850.

ply with these rules. An American whaler, Charles Brower, wrote the following account of the conflicting norms in 1886:

> In everything we did, the Inuit found fault with, saying if we did thus and so the whales would never come along the ice. First they objected to our hammering after the sun came up, the whales would hear us, whales could hear a long distance. Our gear was wrong; they had never used that kind, it was forbidden. Tents were out of the question, as for cooking on the ice, that was not to be thought of. When they found out we were getting extra footgear to take with us, that was the limit, then they knew we would never get a whale.

As contacts between the Inuit and Europeans and Americans increased, the Inuit began to shift their economic activities to trapping, whaling, and trading with the foreigners. They altered their seasonal settlement patterns in favor of greater stability near coastal and inland trading posts.

And, as in other Arctic regions, Alaskan Inuit suffered from deadly epidemics introduced into their territory by European carriers. Several devastating epidemics of influenza and measles struck Inuit communities in the second half of the 19th century. Many people died and in some cases entire settlements were destroyed.

In 1867, the United States government purchased the territory of Alaska from the Russians. The Russian-American Company was bought out by an American firm known as the Alaska Commercial Company. The new company continued the trading networks already in place. American merchants operated trading posts and expanded contacts with the Inuit throughout the later years of the 19th century.

Commercial whaling also continued and in some areas increased due to the

BOUNDARY LINE ON CHILKOOT PASS

Prospectors prepare to cross the Chilkoot Pass to the gold rush country of the Klondike in 1898. The discovery of gold at many different sites in Alaska brought a new influx of immigrants to that territory, resulting in even greater pressure on the Inuit way of life.

fact that after 1880, American whalers began to winter in Alaska rather than return south after the brief summer season. They stayed in protected harbors along the coast and also founded two major whaling stations in Alaska, one at Barrow Point in 1884 and the second at Point Hope in 1887. Some Inuit living nearby were employed on the ships and at the whaling stations.

In addition to the Inuit's participation in whaling and trapping, the Inuit worked in the commercial salmon industry that developed in Alaska in the 1880s. Fisheries and canneries were first opened along the shores of Bristol Bay. Inuit men and women worked in the canneries and received pay in cash that they then used to purchase European and American products at trading posts.

After gold was discovered in the Klondike region of Alaska in the late 1800s, American prospectors came to the territory. The Inuit were not involved in gold mining, but those natives living near mining areas had another source of contact with American goods and American culture.

The activities of European and American missionaries also affected Alaskan and Canadian Inuit in the 19th century. The missionaries wanted to convert the natives to Christianity. In Alaska, ministers from the Russian Orthodox Church began their activities among the Inuit during the early 1800s when they arrived with Russian traders and explorers. The first contact between priests and the Inuit took place in 1818 along the shores of Bristol Bay.

Russian Orthodox missionaries followed policies set forth by church officials in Russia. Missionaries were instructed to respect the customs and cultures of native peoples. They learned native languages and translated the Bible and other religious texts into the Inuit language.

Russian Orthodox priests opened schools in some coastal Inuit communities in the 1840s. In 1845, priests established a seminary in the town of Sitka to train Aleut and Inuit converts to become members of the clergy so that they could expand missionary work among their own people.

During the final period of Russian rule in Alaska, mission schools increased their activities in Inuit communities. Most church schools offered only elementary instruction although a few provided more advanced education.

In addition to missions and schools, Russian Orthodox clergy operated health clinics in Inuit communities. They gave basic medical care and tried to improve health and sanitary conditions.

After the territory of Alaska was sold by Russia to the United States in 1867, many Russian Orthodox clergy returned to their home country. Some, however, remained among the Inuit and continued their missionary, educational, and medical activities.

Once Alaska became a possession of the United States, American missionaries from several Protestant sects began efforts to convert the Inuit to their religions. Presbyterians, Moravians, Congregationalists, and Episcopalians

(continued on page 81)

BEHIND THE MASK

Made from wood, sometimes decorated with feathers or fur, and adorned with ivory, the elaborate masks fashioned by the various Alaskan Inuit peoples were primarily religious in function, in that they served to express the Inuit's understanding of the complex ways in which the world operated and of the powers that controlled it. Not surprisingly for a people so dependent for their individual and collective survival upon meat taken from the hunt, the masks depicted the relationship between human beings and animals and between all things and the spirit world. In the Inuit worldview, humans and animals existed in a complex reciprocal relationship in which animals gave themselves to the hunter in response to the respect with which the people treated them.

To celebrate the end of the whaling season, North Alaskan Inuit hunters would dance from house to house wearing masks and breastplates such as the ones seen here.

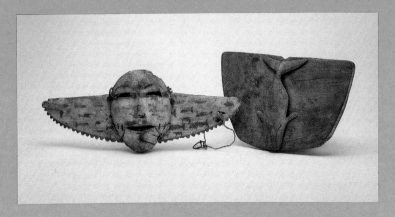

A spotted mask of the Bering Sea Inuit. Spots or dots were a motif in many Inuit ceremonial objects and rituals. They were probably intended to call to mind circles or eyes, both of which symbolized spiritual awareness and insight and the connection between the material and spirit worlds.

This mask is intended to represent the face of a grizzly bear spirit as it eats a salmon, one of its favorite foods. Made of wood, the concentric hoops around the face are called ellanguat and are intended to represent the cosmos, or universe.

The black marks on the chin and across the eyes of this North Alaskan Inuit mask were known as the mark of the whale man and signified the wearer's prowess in that pursuit.

The Inuit believed that humans, animals, and indeed all things possess immortal souls, and that animals and humans are able to transform themselves from one into the other. These items crafted by the Bering Sea Inuit were worn as jewelry. The larger object is a hair ornament; the image on it represents Tunghak, the spirit-keeper of animals in Bering Sea Inuit mythology. The smaller object is an earring, decorated to suggest the transformation of a seal into a human.

Part animal and part human, Tunghak was ferocious and powerful. The circular holes in the hands of this Tunghak mask signify the hole in the Sky World through which Tunghak released animals to repopulate the earth. Though they called the spirit by different names, most Alaskan Inuit peoples believed in a spirit-keeper of the animals.

Through its use of orbs and crescents, this Tunghak mask is intended to call to mind the moon. Bering Sea Inuit believed that Tunghak resided on the moon, and their shamans journeyed there to plead for his favor. Journeying to the moon was also a euphemism for sexual intercourse.

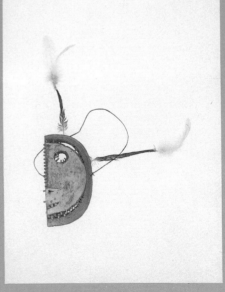

Masks such as this were used for religious ceremonies by the Norton Sound Inuit and were probably intended to suggest transformation.

Pacific Inuit masks such as this one often depicted beings with high foreheads. The exact significance of such images is not known, though some archaeologists believe such masks were intended to portray evil spirits.

(continued from page 72)

competed for influence among the natives. They each founded missions and opened schools for Inuit children.

In 1884, the U.S. Congress passed the Alaska Organic Act that established a territorial government based in the town of Sitka. The act stated that the government should not interfere with the natives' traditional uses of land and sea resources. But it did allow interference in native cultural practices. It mandated education for Inuit and Aleut children to persuade them to give up their traditional beliefs and customs.

Educational goals were clearly stated by the United States commissioner of education, who said that "schools should provide such education as to prepare the natives to take up the industries and modes of life established in the States by our white population, and by all means not try to continue their tribal life."

Then, in 1885, the U.S. government appointed a Presbyterian minister, Sheldon Jackson, to be superintendent of education in Alaska. At that time, all Alaskan schools were operated by church groups. Jackson proceeded to divide Alaska into regional sections, each under the control of a specific American Protestant church.

Although the Russian Orthodox clergy were kept from participating in Jackson's scheme, they continued to run private church schools in some Inuit communities. And in several cases, they actively defended the Inuit against abuse by traders and government agents. In 1897, Bishop Nikolai of Alaska sent a letter to U.S. president William McKinley to protest fraudulent actions by merchants of the Alaska Commercial Company. Nikolai also criticized the educational policies of Superintendent Jackson.

In the Canadian Arctic, missionary activity began in the late 18th century. Moravians were the first church group to make a concerted effort to convert the Inuit. They started work among the Inuit along the eastern coast of Labrador and Quebec in 1771. Their earliest attempts met with little success and were soon abandoned. However, Moravian missions increased in the 19th century as ministers traveled into the interior of the Canadian Arctic.

In addition to churches, Moravians operated stores and thus competed with commercial trading companies. Moravians were often successful in attracting business from the Inuit and gained influence in Inuit communities.

By the middle of the 19th century, Anglican missionaries started to work among the Inuit in Quebec. Roman Catholics came to the Arctic as well. At first, none of the Christian groups had much effect on Inuit society, but once they began to operate schools in the Canadian Arctic in the late 19th century, they increased their influence among the native peoples.

The 19th century, then, was a time of growing contact between the Inuit and Europeans, Americans, and Canadians. As contact expanded from trade to education to health care to religion, changes in Inuit lifeways increased. ▲

In traditional Inuit belief, a child's name carries with it aspects of the sacred. Children were generally named after an ancestor, and the naming imparted part of the ancestor's soul to the newborn.

ADJUSTING TO CHANGE

The lives of the Inuit changed dramatically in the 20th century. Trends that had begun gradually in earlier years grew stronger. The people became more dependent on goods obtained from Canadian and American traders. Technological changes took place in Inuit culture as the people replaced traditional tools, utensils, and weapons with those they received through trade. And changes occurred in Inuit society as trade and wagework replaced traditional subsistence activities.

These shifts in Inuit culture took place throughout the Arctic although the degree of change varied among different groups. For people living in Alaska and along the eastern coast of Labrador and Quebec, technological and social alterations were well underway by the beginning of the 20th century. For the Inuit living in the central Canadian Arctic, initial contact with traders, missionaries, and government agents did not occur until the early years of the century and therefore traditional practices continued

for a far longer period of time. Indeed, in some central regions, the lives of the Inuit were essentially unchanged until the 1940s.

In Alaska, important economic changes occurred around the turn of the 20th century when the commercial whaling industry declined. The demand for whale oil disappeared due to the discovery of petroleum in the state of Pennsylvania in the 1860s. And the demand for baleen also sharply diminished because of several factors. In the late 19th century, the price of baleen soared as the number of whales declined due to overkill. Because of high prices, American and European industries that used baleen tried to find a cheaper substitute. They replaced it with rubber molded over a thin piece of steel. Once this process was perfected, commercial whaling was no longer profitable and the whalers ended their operations in the Arctic.

When the whalers left the Arctic, the Inuit who had traded with them or worked for them found themselves in a difficult situation. The people had come to depend on the whalers to supply them with manufactured goods. And many Inuit had worked aboard whaling ships or at coastal whaling stations, receiving wages in goods or cash.

But as whaling declined, another economic opportunity arose. Canadian, American, and European merchants were interested in obtaining furs of Arctic animals, especially fox and mink. The Inuit then shifted from whaling to trapping as a means of livelihood. They brought furs to trading posts and received goods and/or money in return.

In some ways it was fortunate for the Inuit that trapping appeared as a replacement for whaling, because the people were able to continue obtaining the manufactured goods that they wanted. But in other ways the rapid shift to trapping covered up a deep problem in the new Inuit economy. The problem was that the Inuit relied on industries that were unstable and unpredictable. Prices for whale products rose and fell due to factors outside the Inuit's control. And prices for animal furs also reacted to external market factors. The Inuit's economic security was therefore uncertain; the people could not affect or control the markets that they depended on.

Yet the Inuit did not want to give up their new ways of life to return to the old. The use of tools and weapons made in North America and Europe vastly improved the success of Inuit hunters. Rifles, steel-headed harpoons, fishnets, and steel fishhooks made hunting and fishing easier and more reliable. People could spend less time in these pursuits and still have greater success.

The ability of Inuit men to bring in a catch affected other aspects of their community life. Since a hunter was more likely to be successful than in the past, he no longer needed cooperation and assistance from other men. It was no longer necessary for several men to hunt collectively at seal breathing holes or for an entire community to cooperate in caribou drives. Since people were able to hunt alone, traditional patterns of food distribution weakened. Rather than sharing one's catch with other members of the settlement, people kept what they caught or distributed it within a much smaller network of relatives.

Trapping also became an individual endeavor. A man worked his traplines by himself. He kept the products received from traders for his own or his family's use.

Whale hunting, of course, continued to be a collective effort, but even this activity changed somewhat from previous times. In the past, members of a whaling crew usually remained together year after year. They formed a stable social network even when the whaling season ended. But in the 20th century, such communal bonds weakened. An umialik recruited men for his whaling crew on a limited seasonal basis.

The decline in cooperative labor and in sharing products with all members of one's community led to a shift in family relations. The nuclear family, consisting of parents and their children, became

Inuit children skip rope. Like most North American native peoples, the Inuit have had to find a way to blend the modern and the traditional.

more important than the larger extended family that had included grandparents, siblings, and their children.

Due to changes in the Inuit's economic activities, people tended to remain in more permanent settlements. Traditional patterns of seasonal migrations and relocations ended. Small villages sprang up around trading posts and administrative centers. Although in comparison with Canadian and American lifestyles these villages were tiny, they were much larger than Inuit settlements of the past. As many as 300 people congregated in a village and remained there throughout the year.

The new pattern of permanent residence made life easier for the Inuit. They no longer had to endure difficult and dangerous journeys from place to place, exposed to the bitter Arctic winters. They did not have to spend time and energy constructing new dwellings. In addition, they could accumulate more material goods since they did not have to pack up and transport their possessions on frequent moves.

But the growth of larger settlements posed some new problems for Inuit society. In the past, social order and cooperation was easily maintained within a small camp. Family leaders served as

In 1952, these Inuit still relied on sleds and dogs to transport them across the frozen spaces of Baffin Island. Today, most Inuit are more likely to rely on snowmobiles.

community leaders on an informal basis. Cooperation among family members was quickly extended to all people within the settlement, most of whom were related in some way.

In the new system, people lived together within a community with others who were strangers. They had no traditional basis for cooperating. And family leaders could not automatically use their influence when disputes or social tensions arose. It took many years for the Inuit to develop their own systems of village leadership and community control.

In Alaska, the U.S. government took a number of steps to assert control over the territory and its inhabitants. As more American settlers came to Alaska, the government extended homestead laws to the region. These laws made it possible for non-natives to obtain "unused" land at very low prices. Most Inuit were not immediately affected by the influx of settlers because they lived in areas away from the growing Alaskan towns and cities. But those Inuit who lived close to American settlements had increased contact with American culture. And this contact with Americans resulted in new waves of epidemic diseases in Inuit communities. Many Inuit died in a devastating epidemic of measles in 1902.

As whaling declined in the early 20th century, and as the number of caribou also diminished due to overkill, the U.S. government introduced reindeer herding to Inuit villagers. American officials hoped that this enterprise would give the Inuit a stable source of income. They also hoped that it would encourage the Inuit to remain in permanent settlements rather than to follow their traditional patterns of seasonal migrations. But reindeer herding never became a secure feature of the Inuit's economic activities. The Inuit were not especially interested in herding and, in any case, several bouts of disease eliminated the majority of the animals provided for them.

In the early years of the century, the American government turned its attention to the schooling of Inuit children. Until that time, all children—Inuit, Aleut, and American—attended schools together in their district. But American settlers complained to officials because they did not want their children at school with the native children. The government responded by segregating the schools in 1905.

Officials wanted to teach Inuit children American practices and values. By so doing, they hoped that the next generation of Inuit would abandon their traditional culture. Educational policy was set forth in a statement from the Alaska Bureau of Education in 1911:

The work of the Bureau of Education, which is conducted for the benefit of adults as well as children, is practical in character, emphasis being placed on the development of domestic industries, household arts, personal hygiene, village sanitation, and the elementary English subjects.

In accordance with this plan, officials stressed the importance of teaching the English language to Inuit children. Schoolchildren were not allowed to speak their own language. The recollections of an Inuit man, John Tetpon, document the policy and its effects. He recalled:

> I'll never forget my first day at school. I had waited for this day for years to enter the white frame building where my two older brothers read books and learned to write their names. I was six years old and didn't know a word of English. Excited, I jabbered away to all my friends in Inupiaq [the native language of the Alaskan Inuit].
>
> From the front of the room, the teacher studied us closely. He was a big man with giant hands, dressed in a white shirt and tie. He walked slowly around the room and suddenly, out of nowhere, his great big hand grabbed me around the neck. He shoved a big bar of soap into my mouth. "No one here will speak Inupiaq," he ordered.

Inuit children were forced to enter the unfamiliar setting of school and use an unfamiliar language from the very start. In the process, they were taught to devalue their own language and culture.

The economic situation of the Alaskan Inuit improved during the 1920s as prices for fox and mink furs rose considerably. Since high prices were paid for furs, more Inuit shifted from subsistence hunting to commercial trapping and trading. But in the 1930s, prices fell sharply as a result of the overall worldwide economic depression. Once again, the Inuit's livelihood became insecure.

The next period of change for the Inuit in Alaska occurred in the 1940s during World War II. At that time, the U.S. government built several military bases in Alaska. Some Inuit obtained employment at the bases, mainly in construction and maintenance of the facilities. But the jobs were temporary and ended shortly after the war when the military closed most of its bases.

In an attempt to gain more control over their own situation, the Inuit began to organize village councils in the 1920s and 1930s. In the late 1930s, the councils adopted constitutions that set forth procedures for decision making and local self-government. However, the actual authority of the village councils and local leaders was limited. They acted under the ultimate authority of the federal commissioner of Indian affairs, head of the Bureau of Indian Affairs (BIA), which itself is a division of the United States Department of the Interior.

Conditions for the Inuit in Canada during the first half of the 20th century were similar to those for the Alaskan Inuit. The people's economic security depended upon developments originating in foreign markets. As in Alaska, commercial whaling declined in the eastern Arctic by the early years of the 20th century. Whaling was replaced by trapping fox and mink furs for trade to Canadian merchants.

The Hudson Bay Company was the primary source of manufactured goods

Inuit children eye a U.S. Coast Guard helicopter that put down near their settlement in the early 1950s. Today, the sight of aircraft would be relatively commonplace in even the remotest areas of the Arctic.

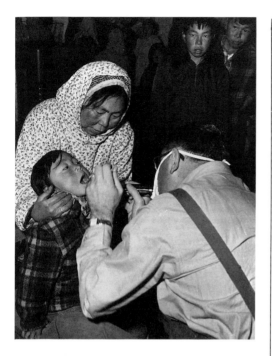

A U.S. Coast Guard dentist examines an Inuit child at a remote Alaskan settlement. Lack of easy access to modern health-care services continues to be a major problem for many Inuit communities.

and tokens rather than in cash. The following system of tokens measured values of animal furs:

white fox:	1 token
blue fox:	2 tokens
silver fox:	15–40 tokens
otter:	4–8 tokens
mink:	1 token
marten:	2 tokens
white bear:	4–10 tokens
caribou:	1/2 token

The Inuit could redeem the tokens only at Hudson Bay Company stores. They therefore were dependent on the company for supplying them with a majority of their tools, weapons, food, and clothing.

Prices for Canadian fox furs rose in the 1920s. At that time, Canadian Inuit were able to obtain a greater number of manufactured goods. In addition to steel tools, traps, fishnets, and rifles, the Inuit got canvas tents, wooden boats, clothing, and some foods such as flour, tea, and sugar. But when the fur market crashed in the 1930s, Inuit trappers and their families were left in a difficult economic situation. They were unable to return to hunting caribou for their subsistence because the caribou herds were greatly diminished due to overkill and to diseases that ravaged the animals. In some areas, the herds were only one-tenth the number they had been in the past. As a result, in Labrador, Quebec, and the Northwest Territories many Inuit suffered periods of starvation and many died.

for the Inuit. Although other trading companies operated in the eastern Arctic, the Hudson Bay Company succeeded in buying most of them out by the 1930s. It then had nearly a complete monopoly over trade with the Inuit. The company expanded its network of trading posts, venturing into remote regions of central Canada. Many Inuit in interior areas then had their first direct contact with Canadian products.

During this period, the Hudson Bay Company paid Inuit trappers in goods

The Canadian government and the Hudson Bay Company responded to the situation by offering temporary financial assistance and food supplies. The government had begun to assert its control over the vast Arctic regions in the early 20th century. They sent members of the Royal Canadian Mounted Police (RCMP) to set up stations throughout Inuit territory. The actual control exerted by the RCMP, however, was minimal. But they did establish contact with some groups and had some influence in settlements nearest to their posts.

The Canadian government also acted to improve health conditions for the Inuit. They opened nursing stations in some communities that offered basic health care services. The people suffered from several epidemic diseases, especially measles, influenza, and tuberculosis. The worldwide influenza epidemic of 1918-19 was especially devastating to the Inuit. In Labrador, for example, one-third of the Inuit population died in a period of only three months.

By the 1940s, Canadian Inuit society had changed considerably from the past. The people tended to settle close to small centers where trading posts, police outposts, and nursing stations were located. Inuit communities were stable throughout the year. People gave up their seasonal migrations as they changed their economy from subsistence hunting to trapping and trading. And the Inuit family structure resembled the nuclear family rather than the extended families of prior times.

After World War II, a new source of income emerged for some Inuit in the northern Arctic. The governments of the United States and Canada began to build a defense system called "Distant Early Warning" (DEW). This system consisted of approximately fifty radar stations spread throughout the Arctic from Alaska to Labrador at a total cost of $600 million. Many Inuit found work in the construction and maintenance of the DEW line.

The Inuit in Alaska and Canada both experienced increased government contact following World War II. In the 1940s, the Canadian government took over the education system in the Arctic that had previously been operated by missions. The government built additional schools and mandated compulsory primary education for Inuit children. They also opened additional nursing stations to give basic medical treatment to the people. Patients with complicated and serious cases were flown out to hospitals in southern Canada. And the government provided family allowances to needy Inuit families and gave financial relief to the poor and elderly.

In the United States in the 1940s, the government instituted a policy of restricting the Inuit's traditional hunting and fishing activities. They set quotas for several species of animals and birds. Hardship and starvation sometimes resulted but even in these cases, Inuit hunters were fined if they violated the rules. An American observer of the period, Charles Brower, complained vociferously to officials about the policy. He wrote:

Inuit adolescents compete at a traditional game in the community hall at Cape Dorset, Alaska, in 1967. Though today they often wear the trappings of modern civilization, many Inuit traditions persist.

There has been no ice here for over a month and so there is no hunting— no seals and no walrus. All the natives are getting hungry. There is plenty of caribou just to the east but the restrictions are so that no one is allowed to kill them.

Now the Department of Interior has issued hunting licenses to the Inuit and every duck, ptarmigan, caribou, moose, or sheep that they kill has to be reported. They have nothing to buy with so all are hard up for meat and clothing. It is pitiful to see the kids around with nothing on but rags.

In 1959, the territory of Alaska was granted statehood. When the new state took over educational services from the federal government, it ended the system of segregated schooling for Inuit children. All children, then, attended the school closest to their homes. But other federal programs continued to affect the Inuit through the Bureau of Indian Affairs. BIA officials encouraged the formation of village councils in all Inuit communities. As in the past, though, the councils did not have full independence but rather operated under the supervision of BIA agents.

By the middle of the 20th century, the Inuit adjusted to alterations in their economic and social activities. They responded by trying to take greater control over their own lives in the wake of changes brought about by outside forces. ▲

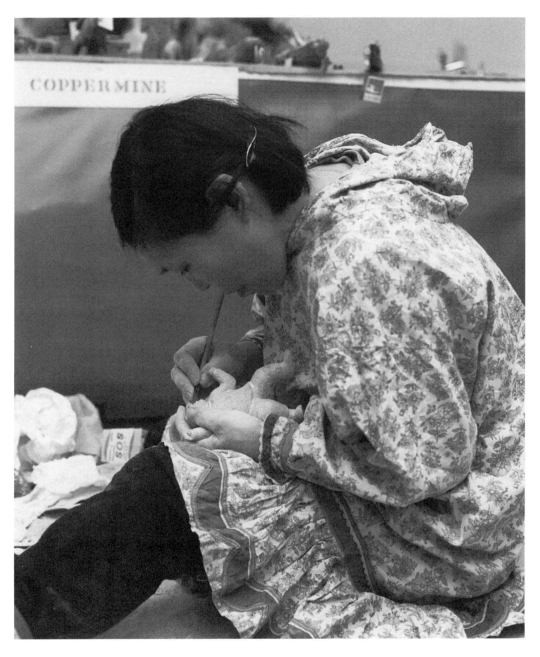

A Canadian Inuit puts the finishing touches on a soapstone carving. Many modern Inuit artists and craftsmen have discovered that their talent can earn them money, although exploitation by dealers and collectors is still commonplace.

THE
INUIT
TODAY

The Inuit in Alaska and Canada today are merging their old traditions with new ways of living. A recent description of the northernmost Alaskan town of Barrow, given by Margaret Blackman, can account for many Arctic communities:

> Barrow's three well-stocked grocery stores notwithstanding, fish and bearded seal meat hang to dry in the summer sun from racks beside the houses. A native student participating in a summer archeology dig misses a day of work to go walrus hunting with his father; an umiak rests upside down next to a plexiglass-covered bus stop. The sleek city buses take shotgun-toting Inuit six miles north of town where enormous flocks of ducks fly to and from their summer feeding grounds. The mayor of Barrow has been a whaling captain, and the former magistrate found time to sew new clothing for members of her husband's whaling crew. The cabs in town may not run in the spring because their drivers are out on the ice, hunting whales.

Since the 1960s, several important developments have taken place in the economic, political, and social lives of the Inuit in Alaska and Canada. One factor was the growth of economic cooperatives in many communities throughout the Arctic. The first such enterprise was founded in 1959 by the Inuit at the river George, a settlement located on the shores of Ungava Bay in northern Quebec. Since then, other cooperatives have been formed all over Canada and Alaska. The cooperatives initially marketed Inuit crafts produced by local artisans. Craftspeople specialize in making soapstone and ivory carvings of animals and human figures. They are continuing a style of artwork dating back to ancestors who lived thousands of years ago. Through the cooperatives, artisans sell their work to galleries and shops in Canada, the United States, and Europe. Craft production is a major source of income for some Inuit. In addition to sculpture, they create paintings, prints, calendars, and embroidered clothing.

Inuit cooperatives also organize local businesses and sell their products. They represent a variety of industries, including lumber mills, bakeries, house and boat construction firms, and canneries for native foods such as char.

Cooperatives are loosely linked to federal and provincial organizations such as the Federation of Cooperatives of New Quebec, founded in 1967. These associations provide helpful information to members about projects undertaken by groups in each locale. Cooperatives have been a boost to Inuit communities because of the economic benefits they supply and because they are an example of how the people can successfully act together to improve their situation.

Economic cooperatives have been organized in Alaska as well. They have formed larger organizations such as the Alaska Native Industries Cooperative Association. Alaskan cooperatives market Inuit products, including artwork, Arctic fish, and lumber. In addition, they operate stores where they sell foods, tools, and household goods at low prices because they are able to purchase them in large quantity from suppliers.

Another economic development in both the Alaskan and Canadian Arctic is the shift to wagework as a primary means of livelihood for many Inuit. This change is perhaps more significant in Alaska than in the Canadian Arctic because large towns and cities in Alaska provide more employment opportunities. In Canada, most communities in Inuit territory are quite small and offer only a limited number of jobs. In Alaska, jobs are available in industries such as construction, lumbering, oil fields, and salmon canneries. Inuit also find employment in service-sector occupations including local businesses, restaurants, and shops. Canadian Inuit can obtain a small number of jobs in their settlements. Most of these jobs are connected to government agencies that provide health, education, social welfare, and police services.

Despite the growth of employment in the Arctic, many Alaskan and Canadian Inuit continue to face the possibility of poverty and hunger. People living in small communities have few job opportunities. According to an Alaskan Inuit man quoted by Norman Chance in his *The Inupiat and Arctic Alaska*, the situation is often bleak:

Again spring is here with us, and work or jobs are pretty dim in our area. Last year, all the men were without work all summer long. It is tough without work and hunting only does not meet our needs. Sometimes we have bad luck even though we hunt. We have to worry what our next meal will be.

There's over 25 men in our village and not even one has work prospects. Only three men have steady jobs in our village—that's the store manager, postmaster, and BIA [Bureau of Indian Affairs] janitor,

DEW (Distant Early Warning) Line stations dot the northern Arctic from western Alaska to Baffin Island and provide radar surveillance to protect the United States from aerial attack. Their construction and maintenance provided employment for many Inuit.

plus one BIA cook. We need help to get work. We should get training for older men without high school education.

In Alaska and Canada, the growth of mining and resource industries since the 1970s has provided jobs for some Inuit but has also aroused controversy. The controversy revolves around claims over rights to land and issues of land management and economic and political self-determination. In the Northwest Territories of Canada, Canadian and multinational companies mine rich supplies of zinc, nickel, and uranium. But

according to Inuit residents, the mining of uranium was disturbing the herds of caribou that the people hunted for their subsistence. In 1979, the Inuit filed a legal suit against the mining companies and the Canadian government in order to prevent further mining. The court ruled against the Inuit, stating that the people had no legal rights to property in the Arctic. The court claimed that property rights had been given by the British monarch, King Charles II, to the Hudson Bay Company in 1670. It said that the Inuit had land-use rights but no land-ownership rights. The court's ruling angered the Inuit. But it had the

Modern Inuit life is a blend of the old and the new. Here, an Inuit woman carries a child on her back in traditional fashion as she inspects a sealskin stretched out to dry outside her home in a modern housing development.

effect of contributing to the growth of the Inuit's movement for political self-determination that had begun in the early 1970s.

In 1970, Inuit representatives founded the Committee for Original People's Entitlement. The Committee's goal was to protect and advance native people's rights in the western Canadian Arctic. The following year, a nationwide group was formed, called the Inuit Tapirisat of Canada (ITC). The ITC united all Inuit, including the people living in the Northwest Territories, Quebec, and Labrador. It worked to better the economic, political, and social welfare of the Inuit.

Then, after a decade of growth of the Inuit movement for self-determination, the ITC urged the Canadian government to hold a plebiscite in the Northwest Territories on a proposal to divide the region into two areas. One division would be called Nunavut, the Inuit word meaning "our land." Nunavut would be controlled by the native Inuit. The second area would remain under provincial and federal control. In 1982, such a plebiscite was held. Eighty-five percent of the Inuit voted in favor of the proposal to establish Nunavut. Euro-Canadians in the Northwest Territories overwhelmingly voted against the proposal.

Following another decade of negotiation, Nunavut was finally created. In 1993, the Northwest Territories were divided into two regions. Nunavut became a separate province under the political control of its Inuit residents.

The industrial use of natural resources in Arctic Quebec has also led to controversy over land and self-determination. In the early 1970s, the Quebec government proposed a plan to build hydroelectric projects in a northern part of the province surrounding James Bay. The James Bay projects included construction of dams on rivers that would result in flooding millions of acres of land and disrupting the migration patterns and life cycles of animals, birds, and fish. Disruptions in wildlife patterns would, in turn, harm the Inuit's subsistence activities. The Inuit, represented by the Northern Quebec Inuit Association, entered negotiations with the provincial government to discuss the James Bay projects and settle the question of the Inuit's right to land in the region.

In 1975, the Inuit and other native people concluded the "James Bay and Northern Quebec Agreement," or the James Bay Agreement, with the Quebec government. In the agreement, the native peoples gave up their right to ownership of land in the area covered by the James Bay hydroelectric projects in exchange for financial compensation. They received $60 million in immediate basic payment and an additional $30 million as an "indemnity on future development."

In the agreement, the government recognized the Inuit's right to control their own political and economic systems. They now have local village councils made up of elected representatives that have control over many social, educational, health, and policing services.

The James Bay Agreement also divided the James Bay region into three sections. Land Category One consists of land where no mineral extraction is permitted without formal permission given by community councils representing every native village. If permission is granted, mining and resource development can proceed after financial compensation is awarded. Land Category Two contains land where the Inuit keep exclusive rights to hunt, fish, and trap. Land Category Three consists of land where the Inuit have no special rights. The government can therefore proceed with resource development projects as it chooses.

Although the James Bay Agreement was approved by an overwhelming majority of Inuit in Quebec, some people objected to it. They formed their own organization, called Inuit Tungavingat Nunami, or "the Inuit who stand up on their land." They continue to work to protect the Inuit's right to the land and to better their economic security.

In Alaska, the discovery of oil in Prudhoe Bay in 1968 has led to far-reaching changes in the Inuit's relationship to their land and resources. After oil was discovered, petroleum companies asked the U.S. government to grant them permits to drill for oil in Alaska. The government could not immediately give leases to the companies because the right of the native peoples to the land had not been resolved. According to the Alaska Statehood Act of 1958, which created the state of Alaska, land was not directly awarded to either natives or non-natives. The act asserted that the state of Alaska had no claim to native land but could select 104 million acres of land from the public domain that were "vacant, unappropriated, or unreserved." The state's share amounted to approximately one-third of the total land in the public domain at that time. The state of Alaska proceeded to claim the best acreage. Disputes between the Inuit, Aleuts, and the state arose because some of the state land was claimed by native peoples.

The conflicts over land rights led to the formation in 1966 of a native organization called the Alaska Federation of Natives (AFN). The AFN met with state and federal officials to negotiate a settlement to land claims in Alaska. The AFN wanted the government to recognize the natives' right to enough land so that they could continue their traditional way of life if they chose to do so. And they wanted fair compensation for land that they agreed to give up. The government wanted to resolve the issue of land claims so that it could proceed with leases to oil companies.

In 1971, an agreement was reached between the concerned parties. The agreement was accepted by the United States Congress and passed as the Alaska Native Claims Settlement Act. The act stated that the natives could select 44 million acres of land in Alaska. They then gave up legal claim to the remainder of the state. In return, the Inuit and other native peoples received financial compensation in the amount of $962.5 million. The money was distributed over a period of 11 years.

The act further ordered the creation of 13 regional corporations and over 200 village corporations in native territories. Native residents of Alaska became shareholders in their local village and regional corporations. Each type of corporation has specific rights and responsibilities. Regional corporations receive cash payments awarded under the Settlement Act. They decide whether to invest the money or distribute it among native shareholders. In addition, each

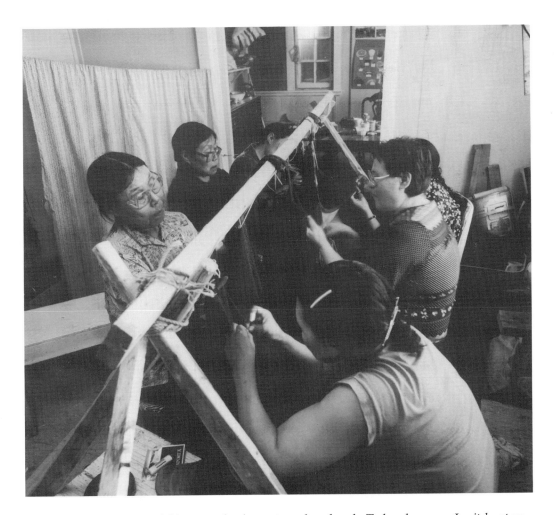

Some Inuit elders sew sealskin around a frame to make a kayak. Today, however, Inuit hunters are more likely to hunt game using a snowmobile and a rifle rather than a kayak and a harpoon.

regional corporation must operate one or more businesses for a profit. Profits are then either reinvested or distributed.

Village corporations also receive cash payments through their regional corporation and operate businesses, but these may be for profit or nonprofit.

Native shareholders receive stock in their village and regional corporations. According to the Settlement Act of 1971, an individual could not sell his or her stock until January 1, 1992. After that date, a native shareholder could sell to anyone if she or he chose to do so. The

Inuit life today encompasses both these traditional-style caribou skin tents, used in a summer encampment in Canada's Northwest Territories, and the huge satellite dish outside of a permanent home in the same region.

lack of restrictions on sales prompted many native people to become concerned about the future possibility of losing control over their land and resources to non-natives. As a result, new regulations have extended the protected period for another 10 years. During this time, shareholders cannot sell their shares although shares can be inherited by relatives in the event of the death of an original shareholder.

In addition to land claims, Inuit in Alaska and Canada have acted to protect their right to hunt and fish as a basic part of their subsistence activities. The Inuit of Quebec have won governmental recognition of their basic economic right through the James Bay Agreement. Inuit in the new land of Nunavut also control their own economies.

In Alaska, the Inuit have been affected by federal and state regulations that restrict or place quotas on hunting and fishing. For example, the Migratory Bird Act of 1916 outlaws the hunting of migratory waterfowl from May through September. But that period is the only season when ducks and geese inhabit the Arctic region. The act therefore denies the Inuit the right to hunt waterfowl even though such hunting is part of their traditional subsistence activities. The unfairness of these regulations was noted by the Inuit and other concerned people. As Reverend John Chambers, a Presbyterian minister in Alaska, noted,

> As it is now the federal government won't let the natives take ducks and geese while the ducks and geese are in the arctic, but after the birds go

south, where they are killed by the thousands by white sportsmen, the government says to the hungry native, "Now you can hunt."

In June of 1961, Inuit residents of Barrow, Alaska, took matters into their own hands. They organized a "duck-in" to dramatize their need to hunt waterfowl and to underscore the injustice of federal and state regulations. Sadie Brower Neakok, then the magistrate of Barrow, recounted the events leading to the "duck-in." In her autobiography, Neakok wrote:

> The Mayor and I had a general meeting with all the people of Barrow. The only way we could solve the problem was for every man, woman, and child that had shot a duck, or gotten a waterfowl, to go and stand in front of the game warden when he made an arrest. And I would know when the game warden would come over and make his complaint and bring that guilty person before me. So each man, woman, and child got a duck from their neighbor, or from the ice cellar, even a year-old duck.
>
> That's how it came about. When the game warden made one arrest, they all went over there. Sure enough, here comes the game warden to my house. He said: "What's the meaning of that crowd in front of my office? Every man, woman, and child standing in front of my door with a duck in their hand."

As a result of the actions of the people of Barrow, the U.S. government

THE ESTABLISHMENT OF NUNAVUT

Communique Issued by the Government of Canada:

May 25, 1993: The final step to conclude a historic agreement between Canada and Aboriginal peoples was taken today. Prime Minister Brian Mulroney, Minister of Indian Affairs Tom Siddon, Northwest Territories Government Leader Nellie Cournoyea, Tungavik Federation of Nunavut President James Eetoolook, and other Inuit leaders formally signed the Nunavut Final Land Claim Agreement.

"The formal signing of the land claim agreement represents a landmark accomplishment in nation building, " Mr. Siddon said. "It finalizes the settlement of the largest land claim agreement in Canada [and] confirms the commitment to create the Nunavut Territory by 1999. It signifies a bold new partnership between Canada and the Inuit of the Northwest Territories."

The agreement gives title to 350,000 square kilometers (136,000 square miles) of land to the Inuit and will provide financial compensation of $1.14 billion, which will be paid over fourteen years.

finally recognized the Inuit's right to hunt waterfowl from May through September.

Inuit throughout the Arctic are determined to control their own education, health care, and social services. They have shaped local education systems to include traditional values and skills. Schools encourage children to learn and use their own Inuit language. And they foster knowledge of and respect for the people's ancient traditions.

Although the lives of Inuit today are different from those of their ancestors, many people understand the value of the old skills. In the autobiography of Sadie Brower Neakok, an Inuit woman who worked as a schoolteacher, social worker, and magistrate in Barrow,

Alaska, she recalled her childhood experiences, first in Barrow and then "outside" in California, where she was educated. When she returned to Barrow in the 1940s and married a traditional hunter, she relearned her Inuit skills. She wrote:

> I marveled at the things that existed up here that I missed in my growing years. I was born into Inuit life, I knew what it consisted of, but I was so young when I was taken out to school. So, I had to learn it all over—learned to sew all over again, how to make clothing, boots, parkas, tan hides. Some of the life of my people just really sank into me because it showed me how much I had missed, and how much I didn't know that existed in our native way of life.

Health problems remain a great concern to the people. The Inuit continue to suffer from several serious illnesses in numbers far exceeding the national averages of Canada and the United States. Measles and influenza claim more lives among the Inuit than among other North American people. And respiratory diseases, including tuberculosis, pneumonia, and bronchitis, are especially prevalent and cause high rates of fatalities among them. The Inuit's health problems are made worse by lack of adequate medical services in their communities. Exposure to cold weather and poor sewage systems also contribute to high rates of respiratory and infectious diseases.

In order to encourage people to become involved in their own communities, many Inuit villages operate radio and television stations that broadcast programs in the Inuit language as well as in English or French. They provide news and information concerning the local, regional, national, and international activities of the Inuit people. And they showcase local musical talent.

Despite many differences among the Inuit in various regions of the vast Arctic territory, the people recognize their common origins and their common problems in the world today. In 1977, the Inuit from throughout the Arctic joined together in forming an organization called the Inuit Circumpolar Conference (ICC). The ICC's goal is to serve as a permanent body for encouraging cooperation and sharing of information among all Inuit. Members can discuss local, national, and international problems, exchange information about projects they are developing, and suggest solutions that can benefit all the people.

And as the Inuit look forward to the future, the words of an Alaskan teenager just graduated from high school can perhaps represent the sentiments and hopes of many:

I see myself getting an education and growing up in a modern town. Because of my heritage and culture, I spend a lot of time thinking about that. I try to mix both together and take the best of the two, and try to be myself too. I don't want to forget about my past culture because of who I am. But I can't go back ten thousand years ago. I've got to go to school and find a job—try to relate it to who I am and what I want to be. ▲

BIBLIOGRAPHY

Arctic. Vol. 5 of *Handbook of North American Indians.* Edited by D. Damas. Washington, D.C.: Smithsonian Institution Press, 1984.

Balikci, Asen. *The Netsilik Eskimo.* Garden City, NY: Natural History Press, 1970.

Blackman, Margaret. *Sadie Brower Neakok: An Inupiaq Woman.* Seattle: University of Washington Press, 1898.

Boas, Franz. *The Central Eskimo.* Lincoln: University of Nebraska Press, 1964.

Briggs, Jean. *Never in Anger: Portrait of an Eskimo Family.* Cambridge: Harvard University Press, 1970.

Chance, Norman. *The Inupiaq and Arctic Alaska.* New York: Holt, Rinehart & Winston, 1990.

Graburn, Nelson. *Eskimos Without Igloos: Social and Economic Development in Sugluk.* Boston: Little, Brown, 1969.

Hearne, Samuel. *Coppermine Journey.* Toronto: Macmillan, 1958.

History of Indian-White Relations. Vol. 4 of *Handbook of North American Indians.* Edited by W. Washburn. Washington, D.C.: Smithsonian Institution Press, 1988.

Hughes, Charles. "The Changing Eskimo World." In *North American Indians in Historical Perspective.* Edited by E. Leacock and N. Lurie. New York: Random House, 1971.

Innis, Harold. *The Fur Trade in Canada.* New Haven, CT: Yale University Press, 1930.

THE INUIT AT A GLANCE

TRIBE   *Inuit*

CULTURE AREA   *Arctic*

GEOGRAPHY   *Arctic Alaska and Arctic Canada in the provinces of Labrador, Quebec, and Nunavut (formerly Northwest Territories)*

LINGUISTIC FAMILY   *Inuit*

CURRENT POPULATION   *Approximately 63,000*

STATUS   *Alaska: members of thirteen regional corporations established by the 1971 Alaska Native Claims Settlement Act Canada: members of native bands in Quebec, Labrador, and Nunavut (formerly Northwest Territories)*

GLOSSARY

Alaska Native Claims Settlement Act The 1971 U.S. federal law that allowed the native peoples of Alaska to choose 44 million acres of land and receive financial settlement for relinquishing rights to the rest. Village corporations with native shareholders were created to distribute the money.

Alaska Organic Act The 1884 resolution of the U.S. Congress to establish a territorial government in Sitka. It prohibited interference with the Inuit's traditional uses of the land and sea but encouraged the use of education to change the tribe's cultural practices.

Aleuts A tribe living on the Aleutian Islands, such as Kodiak Island, in the Bering Strait.

amulet A charm worn to provide luck, success, or protection. The Inuit believe that following certain rules and rituals pleases the spirit world and ensures good fortune.

Bureau of Indian Affairs (BIA) A federal government agency, now within the Department of the Interior, founded to manage relations with Native American tribes.

cooperative An enterprise owned and operated by a group of individuals. Cooperatives of Inuit craftspeople have been particularly successful but a variety of industries have benefited from community economic action.

culture The learned behavior of humans; nonbiological, socially taught activities; the way of life of a group of people.

igloo A winter house for one or two families that is constructed of thick blocks of ice shaped into an insulated, oval structure.

James Bay Agreement A 1975 treaty between the Inuit and the Quebec government that spelled out the Inuit's land rights more clearly; the Canadian Inuit received the right to control their political and economic systems and gave up their rights to specific land in exchange for financial compensation.

kayak A boat, made of whalebone and wood tightly sealed with sealskin, for one or two people.

Nunavut A province, whose name means "our people," created in 1993 in the Northwest Territories and controlled by the Canadian Inuit.

plebiscite A direct vote in which the entire people are asked to decide an issue.

Sedna An important goddess in the Inuit religion who lives at the bottom of the sea and controls the supply of the sea animals that the Inuit hunt.

shaman The individual who treats both physical and spiritual illnesses, provides protection from harmful spirits, predicts the future, and brings messages to the Inuit from the supernatural world.

tribe A society consisting of several separate communities united by kinship, culture, language, and other social institutions, including clans, religious organizations, and warrior societies.

tundra A treeless, frozen area that lies between the ice cap and the forest line of arctic regions.

umiak A whaling boat made of driftwood and whalebone and steered by paddles.

umialik A whaling-crew leader who owns the equipment needed to hunt sea animals and organizes the excursion.

INDEX

NANCY BONVILLAIN has a Ph.D. in anthropology from Columbia University. Dr. Bonvillain has written a grammar book and dictionary of the Mohawk language as well as *The Huron* (1989), *The Mohawk* (1992), *The Hopi,* and *Black Hawk* (1994) for Chelsea House. She has recently finished work on *Women and Men: Cultural Constructs of Gender.*

FRANK W. PORTER III, general editor of INDIANS OF NORTH AMERICA, is director of the Chelsea House Foundation for American Indian Studies. He holds a B.A., M.A., and Ph.D. from the University of Maryland. He has done extensive research concerning the Indians of Maryland and Delaware and is the author of numerous articles on their history, archaeology, geography, and ethnography. He was formerly director of the Maryland Commission on Indian Affairs and American Indian Research and Resource Institute, Gettysburg, Pennsylvania, and he has received grants from the Delaware Humanities Forum, the Maryland Committee for the Humanities, the Ford Foundation, and the National Endowment for the Humanities, among others. Dr. Porter is the author of *The Bureau of Indian Affairs* in the Chelsea House KNOW YOUR GOVERNMENT series.

PICTURE CREDITS

Arctic Program, National Museum of Natural History, Smithsonian Institution: cover, pp. 74, 75, 76, 77, 78, 80; Department of Library Services, American Museum of Natural History: pp. 16 (neg. #42119), 24 (neg. #329639); © Bob Firth: pp. 15, 101, 102 (bottom); Glenbow-Alberta Institute, Calgary, Alta.: pp. 18 (neg. #NC1-827), 34 (neg. #ND1-191); Industry, Science and Technology Canada: p. 94; Karpan Photo: pp. 97, 102 (top); Library of Congress: pp. 26 (neg. #50827), 30 (neg. #68747), 35, 36 (neg. #67382), 38 (neg. #89843), 41 (neg. #13912), 42 (neg. #107327), 44 (neg. #1107281), 47 (neg. #46825), 48 (neg. #107288), 52 (neg. #66041), 54 (neg. #180234), 57 (neg. #38672), 62, 64 (neg. #101193), 70 (neg. #48393), 82 (neg. #109501), 86 (neg. #97366), 89 (neg. #97365), 90 (neg. #85384); National Anthropological Archives, Smithsonian Institution: pp. 12, 68; National Archives of Canada: p. 71; National Museums of Canada: pp. 21, 37; Osborne/NWT Archives: p. 85 (N90-006:0415); Public Archives of Canada, Ottawa: p. 29 (neg. #PA129869); Smith/NWT Archives: pp. 92 (N91-028:0053), 98 (N91-028:0396); Smithsonian Institution: pp. 50, 67; Smithsonian Institution, F. W. Nelsson, 1881: p. 33; Special Collections Division, University of Washington Libraries: pp. 58 (neg. #UW8957), 61 (neg. #UW13557).
Map (p. 2) by Gary Tong.